Stitching
Beaded Jewelry

Stitching
Beaded Jewelry

Lesley Weiss

KALMBACH BOOKS

Contents

Kalmbach Books
21027 Crossroads Circle
Waukesha, Wisconsin 53186
www.Kalmbach.com/Books

© 2010 Lesley Weiss

Photography © 2010 Kalmbach Books

Published in 2010
16 15 14 13 12   4 5 6 7 8

Manufactured in the United States of America

ISBN: 978-0-87116-412-4

Publisher's Cataloging-in-Publication Data
Weiss, Lesley.
  Stitching beaded jewelry / Lesley Weiss.

   p. : ill. ; cm.—(The absolute beginners guide)

  "Everything you need to know to get started."—Cover.
  ISBN: 978-0-87116-412-4

  1. Beadwork—Handbooks, manuals, etc.
  2. Jewelry making—Handbooks, manuals, etc. I. Title.

TT860 .W35 2010
745.594/2

Introduction

I'M GOING TO WARN YOU right now, at the beginning: Beading is addictive. It allows you to take pretty little bits and pieces and combine them to create something completely different. And getting started is easy and inexpensive—in most cases, all you need are some beads, a needle, thread, and scissors, and you're ready to go.

Yet bead stitching can seem a little intimidating at first. After all,

with so many beads to choose from, how do you know what to use?

And what about all those diagrams?

What if the **thread** breaks?

Don't worry. We've made it easy for you to get started, with an overview of all the types of beads you'll find in this book (and in most bead and craft stores), and a simple, visual guide to the tools and materials you'll need and where they'll come in handy. Throughout the book, you'll find tips and advice to help you along.

The easiest way to learn to stitch with beads is to jump right in and try it. This book features 27 projects designed to teach you 11 of the most common beading stitches. Each project breaks the stitch into easy-to-understand steps, with photos and illustrations to guide you. Each subsequent project builds on the one before, so you'll learn new skills with every project you make.

Best of all, as you bead, you'll see how enjoyable making stitched jewelry can be. The process can be rhythmic and relaxing, or exciting and challenging—it's all up to you. Beading is a very adaptable hobby. You can customize it to fit your skills, your budget, and your tastes. With this book, you'll learn the basics as you create jewelry that's as fun to make as it is to wear.

So, let's get started!

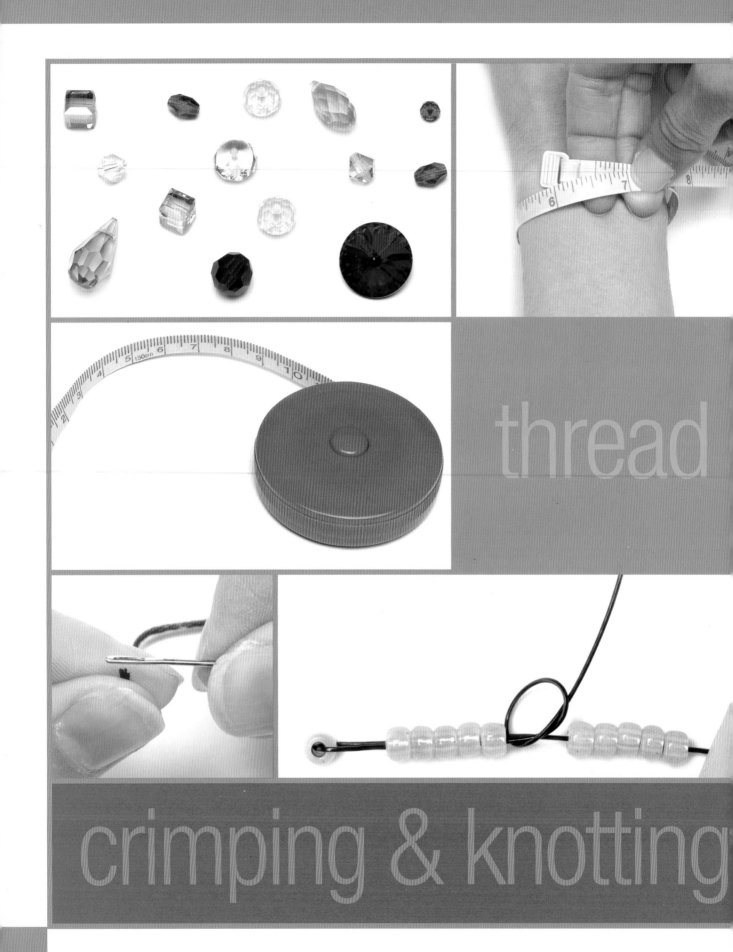

thread

crimping & knotting

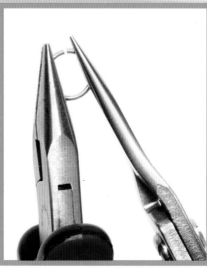

beads

Basics

You don't need much to start making stitched jewelry: Beads, needles, thread, and cutters of some sort will do for most projects. But how do you know what to buy? Walking into a bead or craft store can be overwhelming, and shopping online multiplies your options enormously. Here, we'll start with the basic materials and tools, and I'll give you some hints on what to look for when you're buying supplies.

We'll start with the beads—those little building blocks that make up the projects in this book. There are thousands of types of beads on the market. Some are used quite often in stitching beaded jewelry, so we'll focus on those.

SEED BEADS

Czech seed beads

Charlottes

Czech seed beads are made in the Czech Republic and sold by the hank. A hank is a group of strands, usually 20 12-in. (30 cm) strands. Czech seed beads are oval and a bit irregular, but they are considered to be high-quality and useful beads. Some varieties you may find are **Charlottes**, which are round with a flat facet on one side that creates a little extra shine. **Three-cuts** are a little longer and more rectangular than typical Czech beads. The three facets of these beads catch the light and sparkle. In general, Czech beads are great for strung projects and for projects where you want a little texture.

Seed beads are the smallest of beads—some are only a millimeter wide. There are a few different shapes and styles available. Quality seed beads are fairly consistent in shape, size, and color.

Japanese seed beads

Japanese seed beads are more regularly shaped than Czech seed beads and slightly squarer in shape. They have large holes and a consistent size that makes them great for stitching projects. These beads are usually sold in tubes or packages by weight.

ee-cut seed beads

Japanese cylinder beads, which are sold under the brand names Delicas, Treasures, or Aikos, are very consistent in shape and size. Unlike the standard round seed bead, they're shaped like little tubes and have very large, round holes and straight sides.

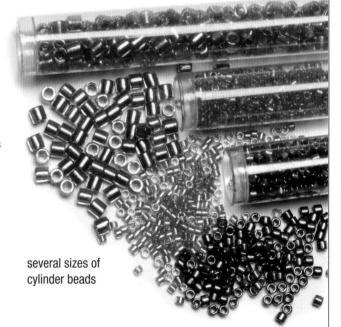

several sizes of cylinder beads

They create an even surface texture when stitched together in beadwork. These beads are also sold in tubes or packages by weight.

There are several Japanese seed bead manufacturers. Although their products are all fine quality, there are some differences in size and shape among brands; you may not want to mix brands in the same project.

OTHER SEED BEAD SHAPES

hex-cut beads

triangle beads

drop beads

cube beads

bugle beads

In addition to round and cylindrical seed beads, there are several other seed bead shapes. These beads can be fun to use because they'll often fit together in interesting ways. **Hex-cut beads** are similar to cylinder beads, but instead of a smooth, round exterior, they have six sides. **Triangle beads** have three sides, and **cube beads** have four. **Bugle beads** are long, thin tubes that can range in size from 2 to 30 mm long. You might also find tiny teardrop-shaped beads, called **drops** or **fringe drops**, and **magatamas**. Magatamas and drops are shaped like teardrops, with the hole through the thin end; magatamas are slightly flatter than drops.

Cube, drop, and bugle beads are sold by size, measured in millimeters (mm), while the other seed beads are measured by aught size. Aught size is designated by /0 or º, so you may see size-11 beads labeled as 11/0 or 11º. The key to understanding bead sizes is remembering the larger the number, the smaller the bead. The aught number roughly corresponds to how many beads fit in an inch when they're stitched together with their holes parallel (see ladder stitch, p. 52). So, for example, eight 8º seed beads fit in an inch. Aught size is a measure of width; you'll find that bead height can vary quite a bit.

HOW MANY BEADS?

1 gram each of six different types of beads

Seed beads are often sold with a label that states weight in **grams (g)**. Supply lists, such as those you'll find in this book, usually tell you how about many grams of seed beads you'll need. (It's impractical to count all the tiny beads used in a project, and bead stores would rather not have you opening tubes to count several hundred beads!) Depending on the type and size of seed bead you buy, the glass used to make the bead, and even the color, the weight of seed beads can vary quite a bit.

The photo above shows 1 g each of six different kinds of beads. See how the amounts vary? Colors, finishes, linings—all these and more are factors in gram weight.

So, you're probably wondering how to figure out how much to buy to make a project, especially if the beads are sold without a gram weight label. I'll admit, it's not an exact science. Your supplier may be able to help you; local bead stores, in particular, have helpful and knowledgeable staffers. Use the materials list as a guide—even bring your book as you're shopping—and always buy more beads than you think you'll need. I buy most of my beads in tubes, and I can usually get a few projects out of a single tube of seed beads. After a while you'll have a stash: your own collection of leftover beads, ready to be used in your next project.

The wonderful thing about seed beads is the variety. You can find so many different shapes, sizes, and colors. You'll see beautiful specialty finishes, beads lined with silver, gold, or vivid color, and even metal beads. Don't be overwhelmed by the selection. As long as you know what type and size of bead you need, you can buy whatever color or finish strikes your fancy.

OTHER BEADS

There are many, many different types of beads. Here, I'll show you the beads (other than seed beads) most commonly used in stitched projects. As you visit bead and craft stores, you'll see other types of beads and get your own ideas for how to use them. That's one of the best things about beading!

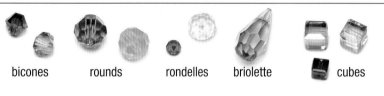

bicones   rounds   rondelles   briolette   cubes

rivoli

Crystals are faceted glass beads that contain a little bit of lead to give them extra sparkle. Crystals are the most popular type of sparkly bead out there, and they're used in a number of the projects in this book. Some of the most popular shapes are **bicones**, **rounds**, **rondelles**, **briolettes**, and **cubes**. You'll also see crystal components that have no hole in them; a **rivoli** is one example.

When stitching with crystals, quality is key—inexpensive crystals can be irregular in shape or have jagged edges. Crystals in general have sharp holes, so pair them with a tough thread or wire.

Fire-polished beads are also very sparkly but less expensive than crystals. These glass beads are heat-treated with a special finish. Oval-shaped rounds and squat rondelles are most common shapes.

Other **glass beads** abound: pressed glass shaped like petals, flowers, or leaves, and other glass shapes, such as bicones, rounds, and pinch beads.

You can find beads made out of precious **gemstones**, such as emeralds and sapphires, and beads made out of less-expensive stones, such as jasper or onyx, in just about any shape imaginable.

Pearls are a classic choice. Freshwater pearls can be surprisingly inexpensive, and their irregular shapes add an organic quality to finished jewelry. If you want precisely matched beads, faux pearls, made of shell or crystal, are a good option.

In **metal beads,** base (nonprecious) or plated metals are economical alternatives, but they may react with skin or change color as they wear. Look for a stamp or label on the beads or package if you want real sterling silver or gold in your jewelry.

FINDINGS

Findings are the components, usually made of metal, used to finish and connect your jewelry pieces. Clasps, jump rings, earring posts, and crimp beads are all types of findings.

Precious metal findings will look beautiful for a long time in your finished jewelry and are least likely to cause any type of reaction with the wearer's skin. The most common precious metal findings are gold-filled, which have a layer of real gold bonded to a base metal, and sterling silver. Base metal findings, made of materials such as copper, brass, and pewter, are widely available and less expensive than precious metal. Here's a guide to some of the basic findings used for the projects in this book.

Clasps fasten the ends of a bracelet or necklace. **Lobster-claw clasps** have a small trigger that moves a little lever. Fasten this inexpensive, secure clasp to a jump ring or loop.

Toggle clasps consist of a bar and a ring. The bar pivots to fit through the ring, then the weight of the jewelry keeps the clasp closed. Toggles are fairly easy to fasten with just one hand, so they're a good choice for bracelets.

Slide-and-tube clasps have one component that slides inside another. They usually have multiple loops, which is great for connections between wide pieces. Some are also magnetic, making them extra secure and easy to use.

A box clasp, sometimes called a filigree clasp, has a spring-lever tongue that slides into the box housing to secure the clasp. Some box clasps have beautiful gemstone adornments.

Hook-and-eye and **S-hook clasps** have a hook that slides into a loop or ring to close.

Earring findings are another important component. You'll most often find **post components**, which usually have a simple loop, or fishhook-shaped **French hook earring wires**. For stitched jewelry, I like to use **kidney ear wires**; the seed-bead loops fit right into the loops on the findings.

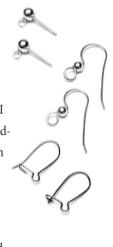

A **headpin** is a short length of wire with a cap or decorative element at the end; you can slide on a bead and make a loop above the bead to create a dangle. **Crimp beads** are tiny metal tubes that can be flattened or folded to secure the ends of flexible beading wire. **Jump rings** are small wire circles that can be opened or closed and linked to other rings or loops.

BEADING THREADS AND WIRE

Choosing the right thread for your stitched project will help give the finished work a long life. If you use a thin nylon thread with heavy gemstone beads, it may break after just a few wearings, and you'll lose all your hard work! This guide will familiarize you with the choices and help you make the best match between beads and thread. **Beading thread** is a wide category. You'll find thread made from natural fibers such as cotton or silk, and from synthetic fibers such as nylon or gel-spun polyethylene (GSP). Most beaders prefer synthetic fibers for stitching because they don't easily fray or break.

In **nylon thread**, you'll have a choice of parallel filaments (a flat thread) or plied filaments (two or more strands woven into a round thread), and several different sizes, from 00 (thinnest) to FF (thickest), with D being the most common. One-G, K.O., Nymo, and C-Lon are popular brands.

One-G and K.O. are preconditioned—they've been stretched and coated with a thread protectant. Nymo and C-Lon can be stretched and conditioned before you start beading. (To condition thread, pull it through Thread Heaven or a bar of beeswax; this protects the thread and makes it less likely to tangle.)

Nylon thread comes in a large range of colors. I like to use flat, preconditioned nylon thread when I'm beading with small seed beads, especially when the thread will show between the stitches. I try to match the color to my beads.

preconditioned
nylon thread

thread
conditioner

beeswax

Flexible beading wire is usually used for stringing beads, but you can use the thinnest wires for stitching as well.

Beading wire is labeled with the diameter (from .010 to .024) and the number of core wires (from 7 to 49). The more core wires, the more flexible the wire (and the higher the price). If you're using beading wire for a stitched project, as in crossweave, it's best to use a very thin wire with a high number of core wires.

GSP thread is made of gel-spun polyethylene. For stitching, especially with small seed beads, **parallel filament thread**, such as Fireline and Wildfire, is best because it's thin and strong. **Plied GSP thread**, such as Power Pro and DandyLine, is a bit thicker and works well for larger beads with larger holes.

Color choice in GSP thread is limited to black/smoke, clear/ white, and bright green. Some black or smoke-colored thread can leave a residue on your hands or beads (easily remedied with a wipe of tissue or Thread Heaven before use). GSP thread is especially good for stitching with beads that have holes with sharp edges, such as crystals. It's also much less likely to fray or tangle than nylon thread.

Because of its origins as fishing line, GSP thread is sold by break weight, indicated by test weight; 4 lb. test is thin and good for small, light beads, while 6 lb. and 8 lb. test weights are better for slightly larger beads. Many bead stores and

online merchants sell small spools of GSP threads, and you can find some, notably Fireline and Power Pro, in larger spools in the fishing aisle of many sporting goods stores. Avoid inexpensive monofilament fishing line; it will often become brittle with time and break.

The bottom line? I recommend that you start with a few neutral colors of size D nylon thread and a dark, 6 lb. test GSP thread. Those options will get you through all the projects that call for beading thread. By the time you stitch the final project, you may have your own favorite.

TOOLS

Beading needles are the most important tool for making stitched jewelry. Beading needles are different from regular sewing needles. They're thinner, more flexible, and usually longer. In beading needles, #10, #12, and #13 are the most common sizes. The #10 is relatively thick, has a big eye, and usually works best with large seed beads (8ºs and 6ºs) and thick thread; the #13 is very thin and great for sewing through really tiny seed beads.

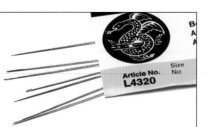

Your needles will get a little bent out of shape as you use them—no problem. That can actually be helpful, allowing you to get into smaller places. It's time to replace your needle when it gets difficult to bead. Don't try to bead with a broken needle—the jagged end can cut your thread.

I recommend that beginners start with #10 needles. As you progress to advanced projects that use smaller beads or require more thread passes through the same beads, you may want to move to thinner needles.

Fine-point scissors or **thread snips** are essential for cutting thread. You need to be able to get into very small places and make precise cuts, so make sure they are sharp. **Wire cutters** are handy as well—use them to cut flexible beading wire and to trim thin metal wire and headpins. I often use the pointed tips of my wire cutters to snip thread as well because they can get into tiny places my scissors and snips can't reach.

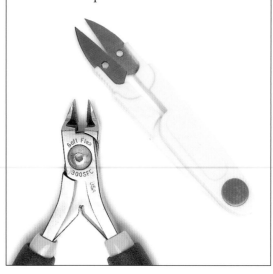

If you work with jump rings, wire, or crimp beads, you'll need a few pairs of **jewelry pliers**.

Chainnose pliers have flat, smooth jaws, and are used to open and close jump rings, make wire loops, and hold components as you work.

Roundnose pliers have cone-shaped tips and are used to form loops and coils of wire.

Crimping pliers are specialized pliers that compress crimps to secure the ends of beading wire.

Other tools that you'll find useful are a **fabric tape measure** for measuring thread, wire, and the finished length of your jewelry, and a **clear ruler** with metric measurements for measuring beads.

You'll want **trays or dishes** for sorting beads as you work—try to find glass dishes, which are less static-inclined than plastic. I like paint trays, little rimless accent plates, and flower-shaped bead dishes.

A **beading mat** made from fleece or Vellux is an ideal surface. It's nubby enough that the beads won't roll away, but smooth enough that you can pick up beads easily.

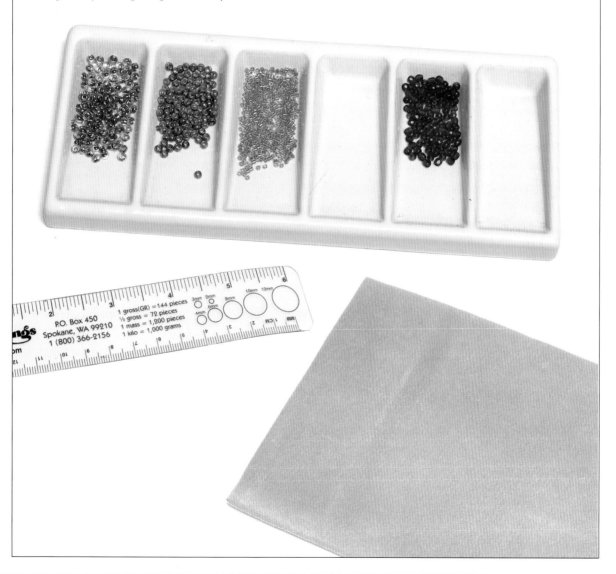

WORK SPACE

Beading is a portable hobby. I know a lot of beaders who bead on lap trays, in a recliner, or while watching TV. Try to find a work surface that's flat and stable where you won't be hunched over. Using a tray or mat keeps the beads from rolling away, and it makes cleanup a breeze.

You don't need to have a dedicated work space. I often bead on a mat at my dining room table, then move the entire project to a drawer or box when it's time for dinner.

When you're working with little beads, good light is essential. Buy a special task lamp for beading or use a desk or reading light. You can find the holes more easily and see the colors more clearly.

As you get more into beading, you'll need to store and organize your stash of beads and supplies. You can find storage containers in all sizes and shapes. I like using plastic pencil boxes for works in progress and small screw-top containers for any odd, loose beads. I keep my seed beads in the tubes they came in so I can identify them if I need to buy more. If you buy bags or hanks of beads, keep the label or tag for the same reason.

And that's it. That's all you need to get started. If you want to cut it down to the essentials, it's as I said at the beginning: beads, needles, thread, cutters, and you're ready to go.

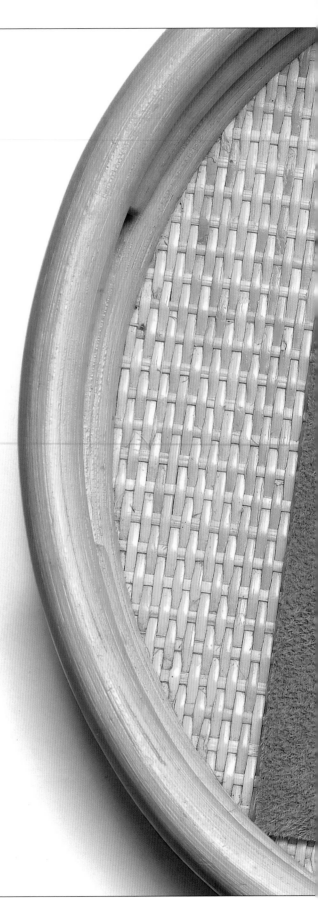

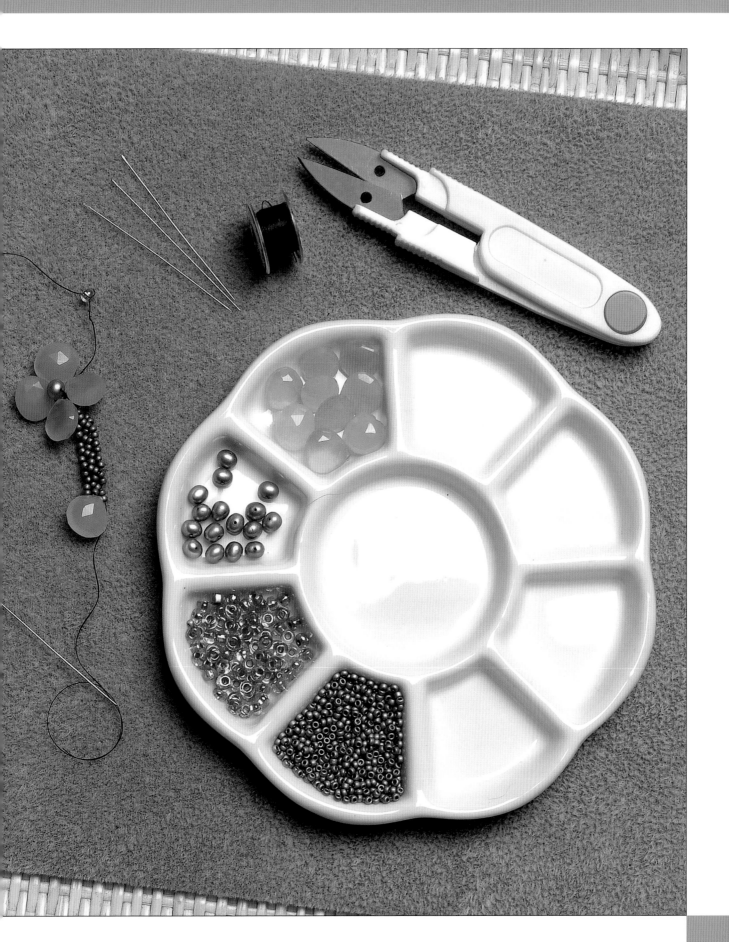

STITCHING TECHNIQUES

Trying to learn a new skill can be confusing. Although I've tried to make the project instructions as beginner friendly and easy to follow as possible, get familiar with these basic techniques and terms first, and you'll be off to a good start.

Getting ready

Get your work space set up, and make sure you have all your materials on hand. Read the instructions through, and look up any terms you don't know (see p. 94).

Measuring project length

You'll see the length or size of most of my projects listed. First, decide if the size works for you. For a bracelet, wrap your fabric tape measure around your wrist. Keep in mind that you might want bracelets to have a little extra room to move. You'll often be stitching to a **desired length** minus an allowance for the length of the clasp you plan to attach.

For a necklace, drape the measuring tape around your neck or measure the length of a favorite necklace you'd like to match. Remember, if you want your bracelet or necklace to be longer than the measurement listed in the instructions, you'll need a few more beads.

Threading the needle

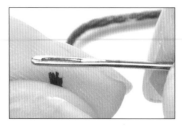

If the project calls for a beading needle and thread, pass at least 5 in. (13 cm) through the eye of the needle. I thread needles using the tailor method: Hold the thread between the thumb and finger of your nondominant hand so you can barely see the thread, and bring the eye of the needle down over the thread. After a little practice, soon you'll be threading the needle on the first try.

How much thread?

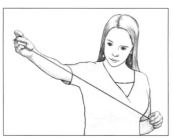

Sometimes the instructions will tell you to cut a **specific length of thread**, which means you'll be able to complete the project without adding more thread. If the project requires a lot of thread (more than you can comfortably stitch with), you'll be instructed to start with a **comfortable length**. What's comfortable depends on you; try an arm's length to start. Longer threads will tangle more often, and you have to pull and pull to complete each stitch. Shorter threads are easier to work with, but you'll need to end and add thread more often. For me, a comfortable length is about 2½ yd. (2.2 m).

Thread tail

When you start the project, you'll often be told to leave a **tail** of thread. Usually this will be about 6 in. (15 cm). The tail has a few purposes: It's handy to hold as you stitch, and you can weave it in after you stitch a few rows so you don't have any bulky knots showing. Sometimes you'll be told to leave a longer length for the tail. This usually means you'll use the tail to attach the clasp. Thread is cheap—don't skimp on tails. Trying to work with thread that's too short is a headache.

stop bead

thread tail

Stop bead

To keep the beads from sliding off the end of your thread, you'll often want to attach a temporary **stop bead**. To make it easy to see, choose a bead that's a different color or size than the beads in your project. Pick up a bead on the threaded needle, and slide the bead down the thread until you have the desired length of tail. Sew through the bead again, making a loop around the wall of the bead. This bead may slide around a little, so for additional security, sew through the bead again. You'll remove this bead later before ending the thread (see below).

Other stitching terms

After you have your thread and needle ready to go, you're ready to stitch. To **pick up** beads means to add new beads by sliding them onto the needle. To **sew through** beads means passing your needle through beads that were added previously. You can see this in the illustrations that accompany the project—new beads that you're picking up will be shown bright and solid, while existing beads that you're sewing through will be faded. If the illustration says to repeat, you may see outlined beads, showing where beads will be added (see p. 39 for an example).

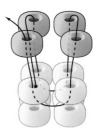

picking up new beads (bright) and sewing through existing beads (faded)

When you finish a project or start to run out of thread, you'll need to **end the thread**. I've used only one technique for this throughout the book so you can master this way of ending thread. To end the thread, remove the stop bead if you have one. Sew back into the beadwork following the thread path of the stitching. This means that the thread travels where it's traveled before. If there's an open space between beads with no thread, don't sew through it when you're ending the thread—sew around it. The idea is to make the thread invisible. Sew back through several rows and around several stitches, and tie **half-hitch knots** (see p. 24) around the thread between beads. As you're sewing back through the beadwork, try to keep your **tension** (the tightness of your thread) loose so your beadwork doesn't buckle. After the thread is secure, pull the end tight, and trim it very close to the beadwork. The thread usually springs back into a bead, hiding the cut end.

good tension

To **add a new thread**, you'll do the opposite: Start with a new length of thread a few rows back from where you left off, leave a short (4 in./10 cm) tail, and sew into the beadwork. Sew through the beadwork for a few rows, following the thread path and tying half-hitch knots around the thread between the beads. Just as in ending the thread, don't let your tension become too tight. Sew through the beads to exit where you left off, and continue stitching. After the new thread is secure, trim the little tail.

tension that's too tight

Sometimes you'll see instructions telling you to sew through loops or stitches again to **reinforce the connection**, often when attaching a clasp or other finding. This means you want to have several passes of thread through the beads and the clasp loop. Clasps undergo a lot of wear and tear; a single thread going through a loop will wear out quickly. I often make four passes through my clasp connection. Try to keep the thread loose through the findings, so the pieces can move freely without sawing against the thread.

KNOTTING AND CRIMPING

There are a few basic knots that every beader should know. In this book, you'll mostly use a half-hitch knot to end thread within the beadwork, but I've included a few other useful knots for your information.

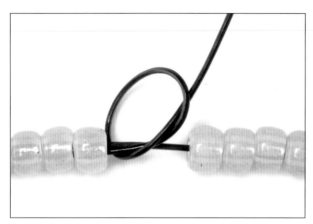

Half-hitch knot

To make this knot, you'll tie a single thread around a second thread that's already taut, usually within your beadwork. Come out of your beadwork between beads, and sew under and over the other thread, forming a loop. Sew through the loop, and pull tight.

The half-hitch is simply an overhand knot tied around another thread. To end or add thread in bead stitching, you'll retrace a thread path and place a couple of these knots at various points (see p. 23). Tighten half-hitch knots slowly so you don't end up with little loops of thread hanging outside your beadwork. I like to sew through the next bead right before my knot is completely tightened; when I pull on the thread and finish tightening the knot, the thread is hidden in the bead.

Overhand knot

Make a loop with your thread, and pass the end through. When you tie an overhand knot around another thread, it's called a half-hitch.

Square knot

This knot requires two threads. Bring the left thread under the right, and pull. Bring the right thread under the left and pull. This knot is often used to make loops of beads, such as in the first stitch of right-angle weave or the first round of tubular peyote stitch.

Surgeon's knot

This knot is a bit more secure than a square knot. It's great for tight spots or when using slick cords, such as elastic. Cross the left thread over the right twice, go through the loop, and pull to tighten. Cross what is now the right thread over the left, go through the loop, and tighten. The extra wrap in the first step locks the knot, making it almost impossible to undo.

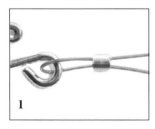
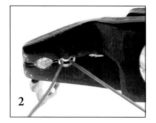
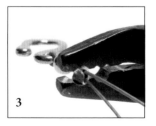
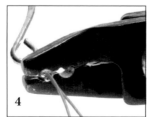

Making a folded crimp

1. String the crimp bead and the loop of the clasp or finding, and go back through the crimp bead, forming a small loop.

2. Place the crimp bead in the half-moon opening of the pliers, making sure the wires are not crossed inside the bead. Close the pliers, and compress the bead.

3. Place the crimp bead in the round opening of the pliers, with the dent toward the outside.

4. Close the pliers and compress the bead into a tight cylinder.

If you don't have crimping pliers handy, an option is to simply **flatten the crimp** with chainnose pliers to secure it, again making sure the wires aren't crossed inside the bead.

WIRE BASICS

Learning a few basic wireworking skills will come in handy as you begin making jewelry; one project in this book (the earrings on p. 34) uses wrapped loops, and many others use jump rings as part of their closure.

1

2

3

4

1

2

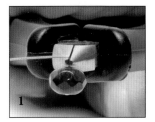

3

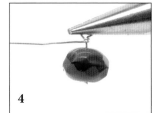

4

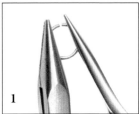

1

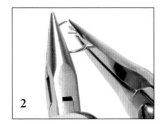

2

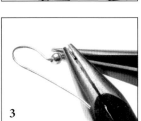

3

Making a plain loop

1. String a bead on a headpin. Trim the wire to ¼ in. (6 mm), and bend it against the bead to make a 90-degree angle.

2. Grasp the very end of the wire with your roundnose pliers, near the tips of the jaws. (The closer to the tips you work, the smaller your loops will be.)

3. Roll the pliers toward the bead, pushing down slightly.

4. Reposition your pliers, and keep rolling toward the bead until the wire forms a circle.

Making a wrapped loop

1. String a bead on a headpin. Make sure you have at least ¾ in. (1.9 cm) of wire above the bead. Holding the wire above the bead with chainnose pliers, make a 90-degree bend above the pliers.

2. Position your roundnose pliers in the bend, so one jaw is in the bend, and the other is on top of it. Wrap the wire around the top jaw of the pliers.

3. Reposition the pliers so the bottom jaw is in the loop, and wrap the wire around the bottom jaw. This is the first half of a wrapped loop. If you want to add jump rings or wires to the loops, do it now.

4. Use chainnose pliers to hold the loop as shown. Using another pair of pliers, grasp the end of the wire, and wrap it around the stem of the loop, moving toward the bead and keeping the wraps tight together. Trim the wire tail.

Opening and closing jump rings and loops

1. Use two pairs of chainnose pliers to hold the jump ring so that the tips of the pliers are on either side of the opening.

2. Rotate one pair of pliers up and the other down. You want to twist the ends of the ring out of the plane, rather than pull them apart. Close jump rings by reversing the motion.

3. You can open and close the loops on earring findings in the same way.

Now that you know a bit about materials, tools, and techniques, you're ready to make your first stitched necklace. Turn the page, and let's start making some jewelry!

peyote
brick stitch

s

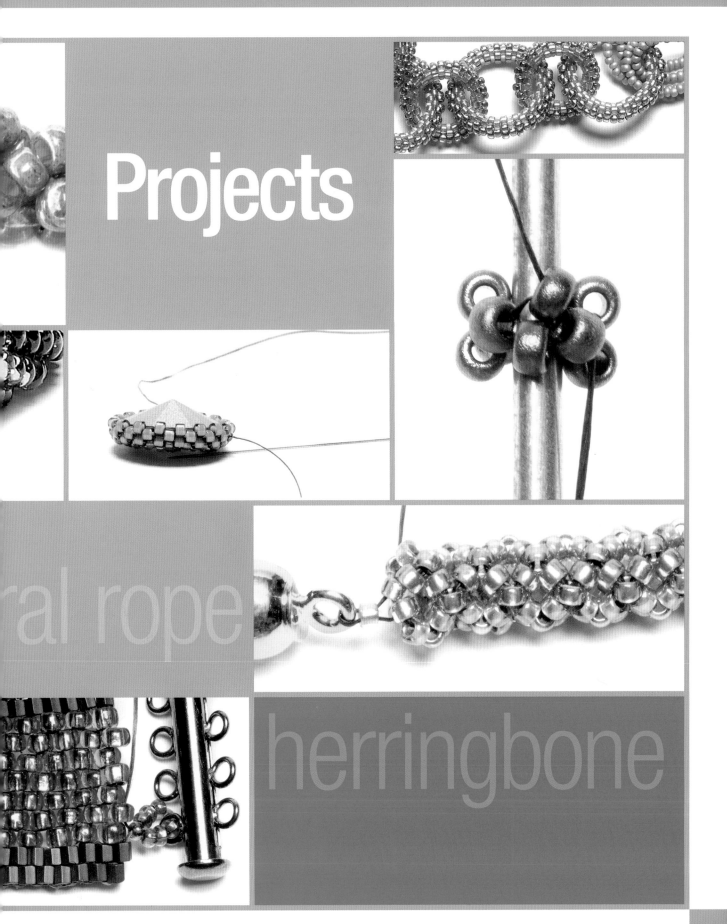

Projects

ral rope

herringbone

PROJECT**1**

Crossweave necklace with pendant

Finished length: 17 in. (43 cm)

MATERIALS & TOOLS

- pendant with front-to-back hole
- 126 6 mm round beads, gemstone or glass
- 3 g (approximately 175) 15° Japanese seed beads
- lobster claw clasp with tag, soldered jump ring, or split ring
- 2 crimp beads
- flexible beading wire, .010
- chainnose pliers
- wire cutters

Materials note
Uniformly shaped round beads fit the boxy shape of this stitch perfectly. You can skip the 15°s if you like, but a little wire will show in each stitch.

This project is an easy step beyond stringing. You'll use beading wire to create a crossweave strand, weaving one side of the necklace at a time as you work from the center out.

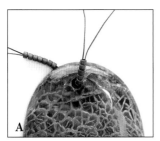

A

B

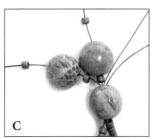

C

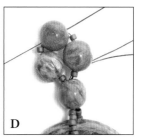

D

1. Cut two 1-yd. (.9 m) lengths of flexible beading wire.

2. With one wire, pick up enough seed beads to fit through the pendant hole, and make a loop. Feed the second wire through the seed beads, and center them. String the pendant over the seed beads [**A**].

3. String a 6 mm round bead over all four ends [**B**].

Push two of the wires to the side. You'll use these wires to make the second half of the necklace.

4. Pick up a seed bead, a 6 mm round bead, and a seed bead on each of the remaining two wires [**C**].

5. On one wire, pick up a 6 mm, and cross the other wire through it in the opposite direction [**D**].

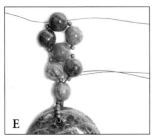

E

F

G

6. Pick up a seed bead, a 6 mm, and a seed bead on each wire, and then cross the wires through a 6 mm [**E**].

Repeat this step until this half of the necklace is about 8 in. (20 cm) long. Snug up the beads so there aren't any gaps, starting at the pendant and working toward the ends.

7. Pick up a seed bead, a 6 mm, and a seed bead on each wire, then string a 6 mm, a crimp bead, and the loop of the clasp over both wires. Take the wires back through the crimp bead, the seed bead, and the 6 mm to make a loop [**F**].

Set this half of the necklace aside.

8. Using one of the two wires left over from step 3, go through the first seed bead and the 6 mm on the top of the necklace [**G**]. Pick up a seed bead.

TIP

A few items are handy for keeping beads secure on one wire or thread as you work with another. Binder clips do the trick, but Bead Stoppers are even better—they are tiny springs that grip the wire. Masking tape also works, but it can leave a sticky residue on the wire.

H

9. On the other wire, pick up a seed bead, a 6 mm, and a seed bead. Pick up a 6 mm with one wire, and cross the other wire through it [**H**].

10. Pick up a seed bead, a 6 mm, and a seed bead on each strand, and cross the wires through another 6 mm. Repeat until the second half of the necklace is the same length as the first.

11. Repeat step 7 on this end, substituting a tag, soldered jump ring, or split ring for the lobster claw clasp.

I

12. Check the length of the necklace. You can adjust the length by removing the clasp halves and crimp beads and adding or removing repeats of the pattern. Replace the crimp beads and clasp halves, if needed.

13. Making sure the wires aren't crossed inside the crimp bead, tightly squeeze the crimp bead with chainnose pliers to flatten it over the wires [**I**] (or make a folded crimp if you prefer). Repeat on the other end of the necklace, and trim the loose wire ends close to the 6 mm.

ANOTHER IDEA

It's very easy to alter this project to match the materials you find. For a large-holed component like this resin pendant, I like the look of a two-strand loop more than a single loop. Center enough seed beads to make a bail on each strand, and then pass all four ends through one large (6–10 mm) round bead. Try creating a pattern using different beads. This pattern alternates 3 mms, 4 mms, and 6 mms in the same crossweave pattern.

PROJECT2
Layered crossweave bracelet

Try your hand at stitching beads with needle and thread. Use crossweave to create a base of sparkling ovals, then embellish the base with a layer of seed beads. You'll be surprised how quickly you can make these bracelets!

Finished length: 7½ in. (19 cm)

MATERIALS & TOOLS

- 70 4 mm oval fire-polished beads
- 4 g 11° seed beads, color A
- 1 g 11° seed beads, color B
- toggle clasp
- GSP beading thread, 8–10 lb. test
- beading needles, #12
- scissors or thread snips

Materials note
Fire-polished beads make a sturdy base, and the sparkle is still visible under the layer of seed beads. You could use one color of seed beads for the second layer, but two colors makes it easy to see where the strands cross.

Because fire-polished beads are fairly large and may have sharp edges, the thicker GSP thread makes a sturdy and secure choice.

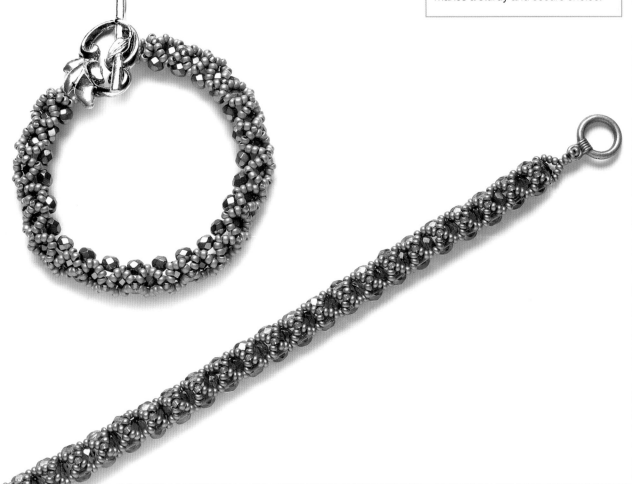

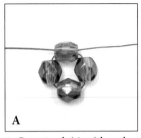

A

1. Cut a 1-yd. (.9 m) length of beading thread, and thread a needle on each end.

2. Center three 4 mm fire-polished beads on the thread. Pick up a 4 mm bead with one needle, and cross the other needle through it in the opposite direction [**A**].

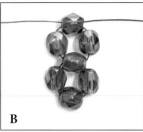

B

3. Pick up a 4 mm on each needle, and cross the needles through another 4 mm [**B**].

Repeat until the base is about 6½ in. (16.5 cm) long, or about 1 in. (2.5 cm) shorter than your desired finished length.

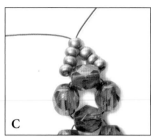

C

4. On each needle, pick up three color-A 11º seed beads. String a color-A 11º over both threads [**C**].

D

5. Pick up three color-A 11ºs on each needle, and cross the needles through the loop of one half of the clasp [**D**].

E

6. Working with one needle at a time, sew through the seed beads in the clasp loop, then cross the threads through the last 4 mm in the base [**E**].

F

7. Pick up three color-A 11ºs on each needle. Pick up a color-B 11º seed bead with one needle, and cross the other needle through it in the opposite direction [**F**].

G

8. Pick up three color-A 11ºs, and cross the threads through the next horizontal 4 mm in the base [**G**]. Notice how the seed beads form an X shape over the square shape of the stitch.

TIP

If your bracelet feels too loose or the Xs aren't sitting nicely over the squares, you can tighten up the bracelet after step 10. Starting at one end of the bracelet and using both needles, sew through the first X unit, crossing the threads through the center 11º as you did before. Instead of sewing through the next horizontal 4 mm bead, sew through the seed beads in the next X. Keep sewing through the Xs, skipping the fire-polished beads until you get to the other end. This will add a curve to your bracelet, so it will hug your wrist. Work step 11 to end the threads.

H

I

9. Repeat steps 7 and 8 [**H**]. Continue stitching the second layer of the bracelet until you reach the other end of the base.

10. Repeat steps 4, 5, and 6 to attach the other half of the clasp. Sew through the next few seed beads with one needle.

11. Make a half-hitch knot: Sew around the thread between seed beads, sew though the loop made by the thread, and slowly pull it tight [**I**]. Sew through the next few beads. Repeat a few times with both threads, following the same thread paths you stitched before to hide the thread. Once you feel the thread is secure, sew through a few more beads, and trim the tails.

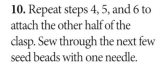

ANOTHER IDEA

These cute little earrings are a great way to use up leftover beads from the bracelet project. It's just one unit of the bracelet pattern.

To make an earring: Cut a 20-in. (50 cm) length of thread, and attach a needle to each end. Work step 2 to create a single square of 4 mms. Skip to steps 4 and 5, picking up the loop on an earring finding instead of a clasp loop. If your loop of 11°s seems too big for your earring finding, pick up fewer beads on each needle before you cross them through the loop. Sew through the 11°s, and cross the needles through the top 4 mm. Work steps 7 and 8 to make an X of 11°s. Flip the earring over, and work steps 7 and 8 again to make an X on the back. End the threads as in step 11. Make a second earring in the same way.

PROJECT3
Beaded-bead earrings

It's surprisingly easy to make dimensional beaded beads using crossweave. String these sparklers on a headpin or earring chain, and finish with a wrapped loop.

MATERIALS & TOOLS

- 24 3 mm bicone crystals (12 per earring)
- 2 11º seed beads (optional)
- GSP beading thread, 6–8 lb. test
- 2 2-in. (5 cm) headpins
- earring findings (hook or chain style)
- beading needles, #12
- chainnose pliers
- roundnose pliers
- scissors or thread snips
- wire cutters

Materials note
Bicones nestle closely together, so the thread won't show much between them. Because crystals can have sharp holes, it's best to use a GSP thread with them.

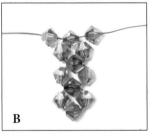

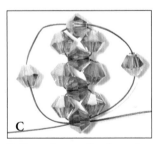

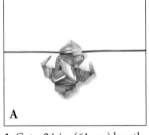

A

B

C

1. Cut a 24-in. (61 cm) length of thread, and thread a needle on each end. Center three 3 mm bicone crystals on the thread. Pick up another 3 mm with one needle, and cross the other needle through it [A].

2. Pick up a 3 mm on each needle and cross the threads through another 3 mm. Repeat once, then pick up a 3 mm on each thread [B].

3. Cross the needles through the 3 mm on the other end of the crossweave strip [C]. Tighten the threads to pull the strip into a cube. You'll have four beads on each side of the cube.

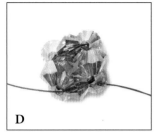

D

E

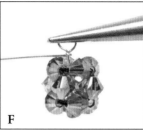

F

G

4. Look closely at your cube. On four sides, the thread passes in a circle between the four beads that make up the sides. Two sides have no thread between the beads. On each of these sides, sew through the four beads [**D**]. Be careful to follow the same thread path through the beads; sew around the circle of beads, not through it.

5. Keep sewing through the beads with each needle, pulling the threads snug. You'll feel the beaded bead getting stiffer as you fill the holes with thread.

When you have about 4–5 in. (10–13 cm) of thread left, begin tying half-hitch knots around the thread between beads [**E**]. You can pull the

knots inside the beads by sewing through the next bead just before your knot is completely tightened. When your threads are secure, trim the thread close to the beads.

6. String the beaded bead on a headpin. If the head of the pin slips through your beaded bead, remove the headpin and string a seed bead first. Using roundnose and chainnose pliers, make a wrapped loop above the beaded bead [**F**]. Trim the wire end.

7. Open the loop on an earring finding. Slide the loop of the beaded bead dangle onto the earring finding loop, and close the loop [**G**].

8. Repeat steps 1–7 to make a second earring.

ANOTHER IDEA

These beaded beads can be used for more than just earrings. Try mixing a few different types of beaded beads together for a bracelet. Work steps 1–5 to make five to nine beads. This 7½-in. (18 cm) bracelet has four beaded beads made with 5 mm round beads and three beaded beads made with 6 mm round beads. The beaded beads are spaced out with a 6 mm bicone crystal, a 5 mm round bead, and a 6 mm bicone between each beaded bead. The bracelet is strung on .018 flexible beading wire, and finished with crimp beads and a lobster claw clasp and tag.

PROJECT4
Square stitch pendant

Pendant 1 x ⅞ in. (2.5 x 2.2 cm)

MATERIALS & TOOLS

- 4 g 10º cylinder beads, color A
- 4 g 10º cylinder beads, color B
- lobster claw clasp with tag, soldered jump ring, or split ring
- 2 crimp beads
- nylon beading thread, size D
- flexible beading wire, .014–.018
- beading needles, #12
- chainnose pliers or crimping pliers
- scissors or thread snips
- wire cutters

Materials note
Cylinder beads have a squared-off shape, so they lock together as you stitch, making them perfect for charted patterns. The large holes of these 10º cylinders allow you to easily pass beading wire through the top row to make the pendant into a necklace.

If you like the idea of making pictures and patterns with beads, square stitch is a great place to start. Square stitch works the beads into a grid, making it perfect for charted patterns. The stitch itself is very simple: Add a bead, sew through the bead below it, and sew through the new bead again. Think of each stitch as making a little circle with thread.

TIP Make your own design! Grab a sheet of graph paper and some colored pencils or markers, and create your own pattern. Don't feel limited by the size of my pendant— go wider, narrower, shorter, or longer if you like.

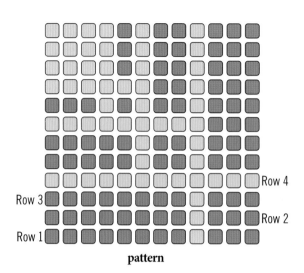

pattern

1. Cut a 1-yd. (.9 m) length of thread, and thread a needle on the end.

2. Attach a stop bead about 6 in. (15 cm) from the end of the thread: Pick up a bead and sew through it again so the thread makes a loop around the outside of the bead. You'll use this tail to end the thread after you've stitched the project.

3. To read the **pattern**, start at the bottom, where Row 1 is marked. You'll alternate direction with each row you finish. You'll work the first row left to right, and the next row right to left. Pick up the beads in the first row: eight color-A 10º cylinder beads, one color-B 10º cylinder bead, and three color-A 10º cylinders.

4. Pick up the first bead of the second row. (Since you'll work this row right to left, the first bead is right above the last bead in the first row.) Sew through the last bead in the first row and the new bead again, so they sit one on top of the other [**fig. 1**]. When you look at the figure, you'll notice that the first row of beads is faded. This indicates that you've already picked up these beads in a previous step.

~Stop bead

fig. 1

5. Referring to the pattern, pick up the next bead in the second row, a color-A cylinder. Sew through the bead below it and the new bead, so your thread travels in a circle and the beads sit one atop the other [**fig. 2, a–b**]. Using the pattern as a reference, keep working across the row in square stitch, picking up one bead for each stitch, then sewing through the next bead in the previous row and the new bead [**fig. 2, b–c**].

fig. 2

6. When you finish the row, pick up the first bead for the third row. Sew through the last bead in the row you just finished and the new bead again. Keep working in square stitch across the row, checking the pattern frequently for reference.

7. When you've finished the last row, end the thread: Sew through a few beads, then tie a half-hitch knot around the thread. Sew through a few more beads, changing direction and sewing through the beads in a different row. Be careful to match the tension of your stitched beadwork; don't pull the thread too tight. Tie a few more half-hitch knots between beads, and trim the end.

8. Remove the stop bead and thread a needle on the tail. Follow the directions in step 7 to end the tail thread.

9. To make a necklace for the pendant, cut a 20-in. (51 cm) length of flexible beading wire, and string the pendant, centering it on the wire. String cylinder beads on each end of the wire until your necklace is about 16 in. (41 cm) long.

10. On one end, string a crimp bead and the loop of the lobster claw clasp. Go back through the crimp bead, and crimp the crimp bead. Repeat on the other end of the necklace with the tag, soldered jump ring, or split ring. Trim the wire ends.

PROJECT5
Dainty square stitch rings

Joining the ends of a stitched strip is as easy as stitching another row: Simply sew through the first row of beads instead of picking up new beads. Adding a three-bead edging (known as a picot trim) hides the thread along the edges of a project and gives it a dressy, lacy look. Square stitch aligns the holes of the beads in each row, making it easy to add trims and embellishments to a finished project.

MATERIALS & TOOLS

- 1–2 g 11º cylinder beads
- 1 g 15º seed beads
- nylon beading thread, size D
- beading needles, #12 or #13
- scissors or thread snips

Materials note
11º cylinders are easy to stitch, yet small enough that the ring fits comfortably. The 15ºs in the trim add a lacy effect without adding bulk.

1. Cut a 1-yd. (.9 m) length of thread, and thread a needle on one end. Attach a stop bead 6 in. (15 cm) from the other end of the thread.

2. Pick up three 11º cylinder beads for the first row. Pick up a cylinder, and sew through the last cylinder in the first row and the new cylinder again so they sit one on top of the other [**fig. 1, a–b**].

fig. 1

3. Pick up a cylinder, and sew through the next cylinder in the previous row and the new cylinder. Repeat to finish the row [**fig. 1, b–c**].

4. Continue working in square stitch as in steps 2 and 3 until the beaded strip is long enough to wrap around your finger.

5. To join the ends to make a ring, sew between the beads in the first and last row using the square-stitch thread path: Line up the ends, and sew through the cylinder above the last cylinder in the last row. Sew through the last cylinder in the last row and the cylinder in the first row again [**fig. 2, a–b**]. Sew through the next cylinder in the first row, the next cylinder in the last row, and the next cylinder in the first row again [**fig. 2, b–c**]. Repeat once more to attach the remaining two beads [**fig. 2, c–d**].

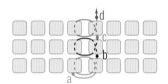

fig. 2

6. To add the picot trim, pick up three 15° seed beads, turn, and sew down the three cylinders in the next row [**fig. 3, a–b**]. Pick up three 15°s, turn, and sew up the three cylinders in the next row [**fig. 3, b–c**]. Repeat until you've circled the band and added a picot trim to both edges.

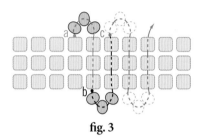

fig. 3

In the illustration, you'll notice that after point c, the outlines of the beads and the thread path are dotted lines instead of solid. This indicates beads to be added.

7. To end the threads, sew through a few cylinders, and tie a half-hitch knot around the thread between the beads. Sew through a few more cylinders, and tie another half-hitch knot. Repeat once or twice more, changing direction. Sew through a few beads, and trim the thread.

8. Remove the stop bead from the tail, and thread a needle on the tail. End the tail thread as in step **7**.

ANOTHER IDEA

Now that you know

how to read charted patterns, try using a pattern for your ring band.

Mix it up with a checkerboard pattern or stripes. You can also play around with the size of the picot beads for a more dramatic look.

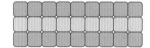

PROJECT6
Right-angle weave basic band

The trick to stitching right-angle weave, often abbreviated as RAW, is to look for the pattern of squares you're creating as you stitch. One stitch equals one square. There's a bead at the top of the square, a bead on either side of the square, and a bead at the bottom of the square. Each square shares side beads with the squares on either side, and the bottom beads of one row become the top beads of the next row. This is another stitch where your thread moves in a circle as you stitch, but here you'll change direction with each new stitch.

MATERIALS

Purple bracelet
Finished length: 7 in. (18 cm)
- 140 7 mm glass bicone beads
- 1 g 15° seed beads
- two-strand toggle clasp (large)

Green bracelet
Finished length: 6¼ in. (15.9 cm)
- 147 5 mm pinch beads
- 1 g 15° seed beads
- two-strand toggle clasp (small)

Both bracelets
- nylon beading thread, size D to match beads, or GSP thread 6–8 lb. test
- beading needles, #12
- scissors or thread snips

Materials note
Pinch beads and bicones work great for right-angle weave because the beads nestle together, making the square shape and straight lines easy to see.

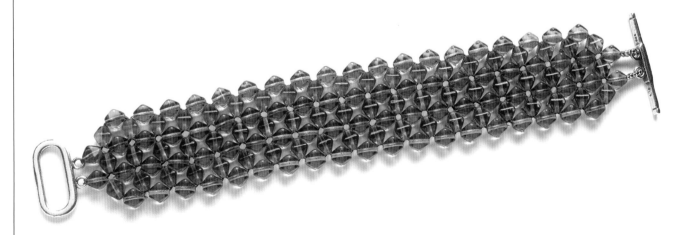

1. Cut a comfortable length of thread, and thread a needle on the end.

2. Pick up four pinch or bicone beads, and slide them down the thread until they are about 10 in. (25 cm) from the end. You'll use this tail to attach the clasp and end the thread later. Sew through the four beads again to make a ring. Pull tight, and sew through the first three beads one more time so that the **working thread** (the end with the needle) is exiting opposite the tail [**fig. 1**].

fig. 1

This is the first stitch. Notice how the beads form a square shape with one bead on the top, the bottom, and each of the sides. The side where the working thread is exiting will be shared with the next stitch. We'll call the bottom beads of the first row the top beads of the second row.

3. Pick up three beads, and sew down through the bead your thread exited again so that the beads form a square [**fig. 2, a–b**]. Sew through the next two beads in the square, so the thread is exiting the other side [**fig. 2, b–c**].

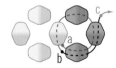

fig. 2

4. Repeat step 3 to add another square to the row. Sew through one more bead, so you are exiting the bottom of the square [**fig. 3**].

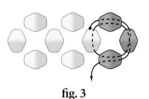

fig. 3

5. Now it's time to start the next row: Pick up three beads, and sew through the bead your thread exited so the beads form a square [**fig. 4, a–b**]. Sew through the next bead so your thread is exiting the side of the new stitch [**fig. 4, b–c**].

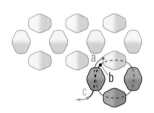

fig. 4

6. The top bead and one side of the next stitch are already in place. Pick up two beads, and sew through the next top bead (the bottom bead of the next stitch in the previous row) and the bead your thread exited [**fig. 5, a–b**]. Sew through the two beads you just added and the top bead of the next stitch [**fig. 5, b–c**].

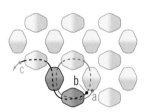

fig. 5

7. Pick up two beads, and sew through the side bead of the previous stitch, the top bead, and the two new beads [**fig. 6**].

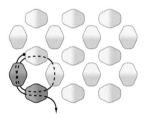

fig. 6

8. You'll start the next row exactly as you did the row you just finished: Repeat step 5, and then work the next two stitches like steps 6 and 7. You can flip the bracelet over so that your stitches match the illustrations.

9. Keep adding rows by repeating steps 5–7 until the bracelet is about 1 in. (2.5 cm) shorter than your desired finished length. End your thread, and add a new one if necessary. Exit the bottom of the last row as though you are about to start a new row.

10. Pick up a pinch bead or bicone, five 15º seed beads, one loop of the toggle bar, and five 15ºs. Slide all the beads up to the bracelet, and sew

back through the pinch bead or bicone you just added [**fig. 7, a–b**].

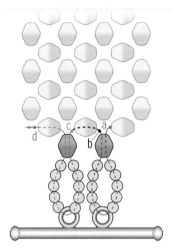

fig. 7

11. Sew through the next end bead in the bracelet [**fig. 7, b–c**]. Repeat step 10 with the other loop on the toggle bar, and sew through the next end bead [**fig. 7, c–d**]. Sew through the stitches and end the clasp loops again. End the thread by sewing through the beads and tying a few half-hitch knots between beads.

12. Attach a needle to the tail thread, and sew through the beads so you exit the beadwork between two end beads. Repeat steps 10 and 11 with the loop end of the clasp. If you like, you can skip the seed beads on this half of the bracelet—the bar needs the seed beads so it can swivel, but the loop can be stable.

Adding thread: a refresher course

Now that you've been stitching awhile, it's a good time to recap this lesson and put theory into practice.

When you have about 5–6 in. (13–15 cm) of thread remaining, sew through the last stitch you finished, following the thread path you stitched earlier. Don't cut across the stitch or sew through open spaces. Every so often, tie a half-hitch knot around the thread between beads. Keep sewing through stitches, changing directions occasionally, and tying half-hitch knots until the thread feels secure.

Cut a new length of thread, thread a needle, and sew into a bead on the edge two or three rows from where you left off, leaving a few inches of tail thread so you have something to hold. Follow the thread path for a few rows, tying a few half-hitch knots along the way. Exit the beadwork where you left off so that you can start the next row. Trim the tail from the new thread after it's secure in the beadwork.

Now that you've learned right-angle weave, it's time to experiment with other beads. It's easiest to learn right-angle weave with bicones or pinch beads because the beads lock together in the shape of the stitch, but you can stitch right-angle weave with just about anything.

Here are some examples using bugle beads, seed beads, and a combination of bugles and seed beads. If you want your band to be wider, add extra stitches to the end of the first row. If you look closely at these bracelets, you'll notice that the stitches don't sit in perfect squares. This is because of the tension in the stitches, and it's almost impossible to avoid.

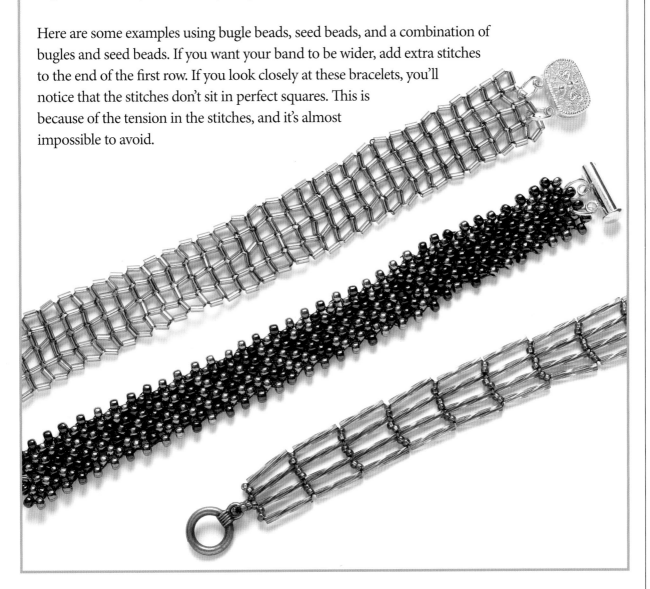

PROJECT 7
Graduated collar

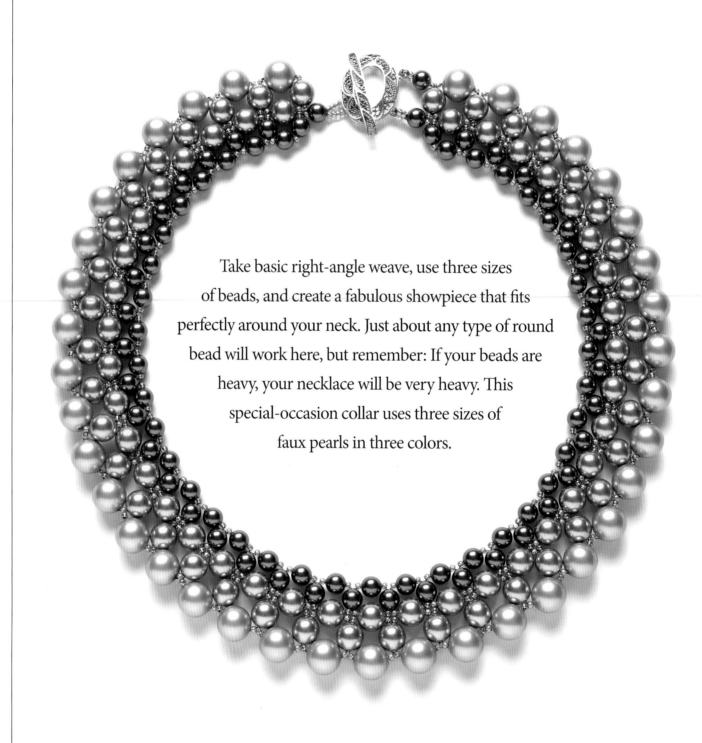

Take basic right-angle weave, use three sizes
of beads, and create a fabulous showpiece that fits
perfectly around your neck. Just about any type of round
bead will work here, but remember: If your beads are
heavy, your necklace will be very heavy. This
special-occasion collar uses three sizes of
faux pearls in three colors.

Finished length: 18½ in. (47 cm)

MATERIALS & TOOLS

- faux, crystal, or shell pearls:
  80 6 mm
  77 8 mm
  38 10 mm
- 4 g 11º seed beads
- 1 g 15º seed beads
- clasp
- GSP thread, 6–8 lb. test
- beading needles, #12
- scissors or thread snips

Materials note

The thread does show a bit when you stitch right-angle weave using round beads, but adding some seed beads as spacers covers the threads. This is one project where you want to invest in a high-quality clasp that coordinates with your necklace. Box claps and toggles work particularly well with the weight of this project.

1. Cut a comfortable length of thread, and thread a needle on one end. Attach a stop bead, leaving a 10-in. (25 cm) tail.

2. Pick up a 6 mm pearl, an 11º seed bead, a 6 mm, an 11º, a 6 mm, an 11º, an 8 mm pearl, and an 11º. Sew through all the beads again to pull them into a square shape. Sew through the first five beads again so that you exit the 6 mm opposite the tail [**fig. 1**].

fig. 1

3. Pick up an 11º, an 8 mm, an 11º, a 6 mm, an 11º, a 6 mm, and an 11º. Sew through the 6 mm your thread exited to make a square [**fig. 2, a–b**]. Continue through the next four beads to exit the 6 mm on the opposite side [**fig. 2, b–c**].

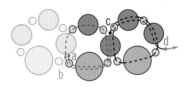

fig. 2

4. Pick up an 11º, a 6 mm, an 11º, a 6 mm, an 11º, an 8 mm, and an 11º. Sew through the 6 mm your thread exited to make a square, and continue through the next four beads to exit the 6 mm on the opposite side of the stitch [**fig. 2, c–d**].

5. Keep stitching in right-angle weave as in steps 3 and 4 until your first row is about 16 in. (41 cm) long, pulling each stitch tight. You'll see the curve start to form after you stitch a few inches. Sew through the beads to exit the 8 mm at the bottom of the last stitch.

6. Pick up an 11º, an 8 mm, an 11º, a 10 mm pearl, an 11º, an 8 mm, and an 11º, and sew through the 8 mm your thread exited to form a square. Continue through the next 11º and 8 mm [**fig. 3**].

fig. 3

7. Pick up an 11º a 10 mm, an 11º, an 8 mm, and an 11º, and sew through the bottom 8 mm in the next stitch [**fig. 4, a–b**]. Pick up an 11º, and sew down through the 8 mm your thread exited [**fig. 4, b–c**]. Continue through the next four beads to exit the 8 mm on the opposite side of the stitch [**fig. 4, c–d**].

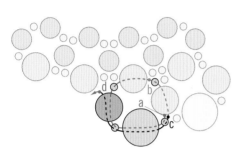

fig. 4

8. Pick up an 11º, and sew through the next top 8 mm [**fig. 5, a–b**]. Pick up an 11º, an 8 mm, an 11º, a 10 mm, and an 11º, and sew up through the side 8 mm your thread exited [**fig. 5, b–c**]. Continue through the next four beads to exit the opposite 8 mm [**fig. 5, c–d**].

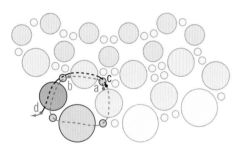

fig. 5

9. Continue working in right-angle weave as in steps 7 and 8, adding an 11º between each of the larger beads, until you complete the row. If you run out of thread, end the thread, and add a new thread.

10. How you attach the clasp to the necklace depends on the type of clasp you have and the number of loops on each half of the clasp. Sew through the beadwork to exit down out of the 6 mm at one end of the necklace. Pick up an 11º, a 6 mm, and enough 15º seed beads to fit through the loop of the clasp. Sew back through the 6 mm, pick up an 11º, and sew through the 8 mm on the end [**fig. 6**].

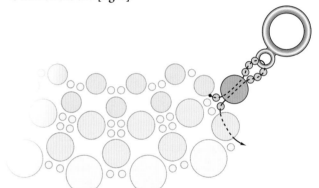

fig. 6

Sew through the beadwork to retrace the thread path through the clasp loop several times. These additional thread passes add security to the connection.

When you are attaching the toggle bar, add enough seed beads to reach from the clasp loop to the end of the toggle bar before adding the loop of 15ºs. If you are attaching a two-strand clasp, add another 6 mm and loop of 15ºs below the 8 mm.

 TIP It's a good idea to think of the 11ºs as spacers in the necklace, rather than as part of the right-angle weave pattern. Remember, the 11ºs are never shared—they belong to one stitch only.

After you've played with different sizes of beads in your projects, you'll come up with all kinds of ideas. These rings are just one row of right-angle weave, but the different sizes and types of beads make them more than just a plain band.

Cut about 24 in. (61 cm) of thread, and leave a long tail (about half the length). Pick up a 4 mm bicone crystal and three 3 mm bicone crystals, and sew through the 4 mm and the first two 3 mms again to form a square. Pick up an 8° seed bead, an 11° seed bead, and an 8°, and sew through the 3 mm your thread exited and the first 8° and 11°. Set aside the working thread, and attach a needle to the tail.

Work the other side of the ring as a mirror image of the first (or turn the ring over and stitch it the same way). Using either thread, stitch in right-angle weave using just 11°s until the ring fits around your finger. For the last stitch, pick up an 11°, sew through the 11° on the other end of the ring, and pick up an 11°. Sew through the 11° your thread exited, and end both threads.

PROJECT8
Daisy chain necklace

If you did any beading as a kid, you may have learned daisy chain. This flowery stitch is a close relative of right-angle weave. It has a square shape, and the thread travels in circles to make each stitch. When you add a bead to the center of the stitch, the square is transformed into a daisy shape.

Finished length 16½ in. (41.9 cm)

MATERIALS & TOOLS

- 8 g 11º seed beads, color A
- 2 g 11º seed beads, color B
- nylon beading thread, size D
- lobster claw clasp with tag, soldered jump ring, or split ring
- beading needles, #12
- scissors or thread snips

Materials note
You can use just about any type or size of bead for daisy chain. Some beads will create a round stitch, while others will stretch it into an oblong shape.

1. Cut a 1-yd. (.9 m) piece of thread, and thread a needle on one end. Attach a stop bead 6 in. (15 cm) from the other end.

2. Pick up eight color-A 11º seed beads, and sew through all of them again to form a ring. Sew through the first two beads one more time [**fig. 1**]. Think of this as a square, with two beads on the top, bottom, and each of the two sides. Your thread is exiting two side beads.

fig. 1

3. Pick up a color-B 11º seed bead. Skip the two color-A beads on top. You want the thread to cross the square on a diagonal, so sew through the two color-A beads on the opposite side, sewing from the bottom to the top [**fig. 2**].

fig. 2

4. Pick up six color-A beads, and sew through the last two color-A beads your thread exited to make a new square. Pick up a color-B bead, cross the stitch on the diagonal, and sew up the two As on the other side of the stitch [**fig. 3**].

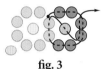

fig. 3

5. Continue working in daisy chain until the necklace is 16 in. (41 cm) long.

6. Pick up two color-A beads, the loop of the lobster claw clasp, and two color-A beads. Sew through the two As your thread exited to make a ring [**fig. 4**]. Sew through all the beads in the ring and the loop twice to make a secure connection. End the thread by sewing back through the beadwork and tying a few half-hitch knots between beads. Trim the thread close to the beads.

fig. 4

7. Remove the stop bead, attach a needle to the tail, and repeat step 6 using a tag, soldered jump ring, or split ring in place of the lobster claw clasp.

ANOTHER IDEA

You can change the weight of your daisy chain by changing the beads. To use a bigger bead in the center, simply add more beads around the edge. This bracelet surrounds 8 mm round beads with sets of 10 3 mm rounds.

On 1 yd. (.9 m) of thread, leave a 10-in. (25 cm) tail, and pick up 10 3 mms. Sew through them all again to form a ring. Sew through the first two 3 mms once more. Pick up an 8 mm round, skip five 3 mms, and sew up through the two 3 mms on the opposite side. Pick up eight 3 mms, and sew up through the two 3 mms your thread exited. Keep stitching in daisy chain until your bracelet is the desired length, minus the length of the clasp. Attach the clasp as in the necklace.

PROJECT9
Big daisy ring

This playful ring uses 12 mm gemstone briolettes to create a large-scale flower as the focal component. When using big beads, you may need to reinforce the initial circle to make sure it will hold its shape.

MATERIALS & TOOLS

- 4 12 mm flat briolettes
- 4–5 mm pearl
- 2 g 11º seed beads
- GSP beading thread
- beading needles, #12 or #13
- scissors or thread snips

Materials note
Gemstone briolettes can have small holes with sharp edges, so using a GSP thread is vital.

1. Cut a 1-yd. (.9 m) piece of thread, and thread a needle on one end.

2. Pick up an 11º seed bead and a briolette four times so you have an alternating pattern of four of each. Slide the beads to the middle of the thread, so you have a long tail. Sew through all the beads again to form a square. Make sure all of the briolette points are together in the center and the thread is exiting a briolette [**fig. 1**].

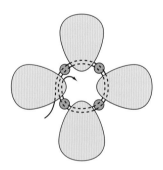

fig. 1

3. Pick up a 4–5 mm pearl, and sew up through the briolette on the other side of the ring [**fig. 2**].

4. Pick up six 11ºs, and sew through the briolette again. Draw the thread tight to pull the seed beads under the briolette. Pick up an 11º, cross the stitch at a diagonal, and sew up through the two

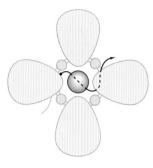

fig. 2

opposite 11ºs in the new ring [**fig. 3**]. (You may find it easier to stitch if you flip the beadwork over.)

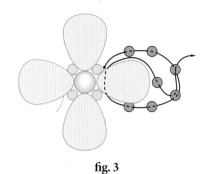

fig. 3

5. Stitch in regular daisy chain, picking up six new 11ºs for each stitch and adding an 11º to the center, as in step 4 [**fig. 4**]. Continue until the band reaches halfway around your finger.

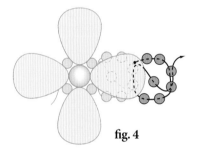

fig. 4

6. Thread a needle on the long tail, making sure you're exiting the briolette opposite the ring band, and start stitching in daisy chain with 11ºs on that side until the ends almost meet around your finger.

7. To join the two ends, pick up two 11ºs, sew down the two 11ºs at the other end of the ring, pick up two 11ºs, and sew up the two 11ºs your thread exited [**fig. 5, a–b**]. Pick up an 11º, cross the stitch at a diagonal, and sew up through the two 11ºs on the other side [**fig. 5, b–c**].

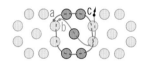

fig. 5

8. End the thread and the tail by weaving them back into the beadwork and tying a few half-hitch knots along the way.

ANOTHER IDEA

Adding briolettes or teardrops

of any size changes the texture of daisy chain. This bracelet features 3 mm teardrops alternating with 15º seed beads for each stitch, with a pearl in the center of the stitch. The stitches still have a flowery shape, but they'll twist and ruffle a little. To make the bracelet, leave a 6-in. (15 cm) tail and pick up a pattern of a 15º and 3 mm drop six times. Sew through the first 15º to make a ring and pick up a pearl. Skip the next five beads and sew up through the 15º

directly across the ring. Pick up a pattern of a 3 mm drop and a 15º five times, pick up a 3 mm, and sew through the 15º your thread exited in the last stitch. Keep stitching in daisy chain until your bracelet is the desired length. Add a clasp as shown in the necklace on p. 48.

PROJECT 10
Ladder stitch earrings

Ladder stitch is most frequently used as a base for other stitches, including herringbone and brick stitch. You can also use this stitch to shape long strands into a variety of playful shapes. These basic double hoops are hung from post earring findings with a few jump rings, so the sparkly seed beads will catch the light as they turn.

MATERIALS & TOOLS

- 4 g 11º cylinder beads
- 4 4 mm oval jump rings
- pair of post earring findings
- nylon beading thread, size D
- beading needles, #12
- 2 pairs of chainnose pliers
- hair spray
- scissors or thread snips

Materials note
The thread is very visible in this type of ladder stitch project. This gives you a great opportunity to play with color. Choose a color that matches your beads or one that contrasts with them to add a little drama to your design.

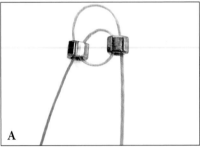

A

1. Cut a 1½-yd. (1.4 m) piece of thread, and thread a needle on one end.

2. Leaving a 6-in. (15 cm) tail, pick up two cylinder beads. Sew through both again, so they sit side by side [**A**].

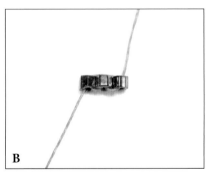

B

3. Pick up a new cylinder. Sew through the previous cylinder and the new cylinder again, so they sit side by side [**B**].

C

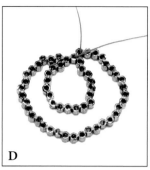

D

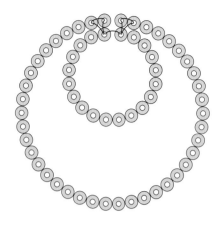

figure

4. Keep working in ladder stitch as in step 3 until your strip has 20 beads. Join the ends into a ring by sewing through the first bead and the last bead so they sit side by side [**C**]. Sew through the two beads again.

5. Now work a ladder stitch strip off the ring you just made: Pick up a new cylinder, and sew through the cylinder your thread exited and the new cylinder again. Keep working in ladder stitch until your second strip makes a large circle around the ring [**D**].

6. Line up the outer ring so the last bead is next to the first bead. Join the end of the strip to the inner ring by sewing through the next bead in the inner ring and the last bead in the outer ring. Secure the join by sewing in a ladder stitch thread path (through both beads twice) between the beads next to the join, as indicated in the **figure**.

Other ways to ladder stitch

Stitching a ladder as described above can create uneven tension, especially when you use round beads. These techniques result in a more-balanced ladder.

Crossweave ladder: Thread a needle on both ends of the thread, and center the first bead. Pick up a bead with one needle, and cross the other needle through it in the other direction. Continue adding beads in ladder stitch until your strip is the desired length [**fig. 1**].

Folding method: Thread a needle, and attach a stop bead. Pick up all the beads you need for the ladder. Fold the last bead back against the second-to-last bead, and sew through the second bead so they stack one on top of the other [**fig. 2**]. Fold the next bead against the second bead, and sew through it. Keep folding the beads into the ladder shape and sewing through them [**fig. 3**] until you reach the end.

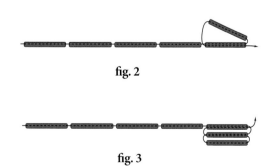

fig. 2

fig. 1

fig. 3

7. To end the thread, first sew through the beads in the outer ring using a ladder stitch thread path. This stiffens the beadwork, so it will hold its shape better. Tie a few half-hitch knots between beads to secure the threads. Attach a needle to the tail, and sew through the beads, tying a few half hitch knots. Trim both threads.

8. Repeat steps 1–7 to make a second earring exactly like the first.

E

9. Carefully shape the earrings and lay them flat on a piece of paper towel. Give each earring a good spritz with the hair spray, and let them dry thoroughly [**E**].

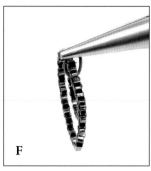

F

10. Using two pairs of chainnose pliers, open an oval jump ring, and attach it to an earring at the top of the hoops [**F**]. Close the jump ring.

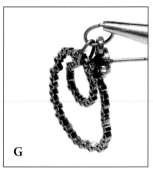

G

11. Open another jump ring, and attach the first jump ring and the loop of an earring finding. Close the jump ring [**G**]. Repeat with the other earring.

ANOTHER IDEA

Have fun designing your own shapes. These flower dangles are a little more complicated than the hoops, but that doesn't mean they're hard.

Start by stitching six beads together as in steps 1–3, and join them into a ring as in step 4. Work a 13-bead strip off the ring, as in step 5, then join it to the next bead in the center ring.

Sew back through the last three beads in the outer loop, and start a new strip of 10 beads. Attach that strip to the next bead in the center ring.

Repeat to keep adding petals until you've worked around the center ring. The last strip will need only seven beads. Attach the end of the strip to the first petal three beads from the center. Finish and spray as you did for the hoop earrings.

PROJECT 11
Striped herringbone bracelet

Finished length: 7 in. (18 cm)

MATERIALS & TOOLS

- 5 g 8º seed beads, color A (light)
- 5 g 8º seed beads, color B (dark)
- 2 g 15º seed beads
- Four-strand clasp (slide or box clasp)
- nylon beading thread, size D
- beading needles, #12
- scissors or thread snips

Materials note
In herringbone, the beads tilt against each other. Round seed beads are easy to work with, but you may also want to try working this stitch with cylinder beads. They give the pattern a nifty, angular look.

See an optional colorway on the bottom of p. 57

Herringbone stitch, sometimes referred to as Ndebele herringbone after the South African tribe that created it, has great texture. You start with a ladder-stitched strip of beads, then work back and forth across the row, adding two beads at a time. The pattern of sewing up and down through the beads tilts the pairs of beads toward each other, creating stacked columns. The striped pattern of this bracelet emphasizes the columns and allows you to play with your favorite colors.

1. Cut a comfortable length of thread, and thread a needle on one end. Attach a stop bead 10 in. (25 cm) from the other end. You'll use the long tail to attach the clasp later.

2. Pick up two color-A 8º seed beads, and sew through them again so that they sit side by side [**fig. 1, a–b**]. Pick up a color-B 8º seed bead, and sew through the second color-A 8º and the new color-B 8º again, so they sit side by side [**fig. 1, b–c**]. Continue working in ladder stitch, and add a color-B 8º, two color-A 8ºs, two color-B 8ºs, and two color-A 8ºs [**fig. 1, c–d**]. Flip the ladder over so the thread is exiting the top of the last bead added.

fig. 1

3. Pick up two color-A 8ºs, and sew down through the next color-A 8º in the previous row [**fig. 2, a–b**].

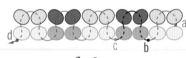

fig. 2

4. Sew up through the next bead in the previous row, a color-B 8º. Pick up two color-B 8ºs, and sew down through the next color-B 8º in the previous row [**fig. 2, b–c**]. Continue working across the row in herringbone stitch, following the color pattern by picking up beads the same color as the bead just exited [**fig. 2, c–d**].

5. To make the turn and start the next row, pick up a color-B 8º, sew around the color-A 8º in the previous row, and sew up through the last color-A 8º in the row you just completed [**fig. 3, a–b**].

fig. 3

6. Work across the row in herringbone stitch as you did in steps 3 and 4, picking up two beads in each stitch, and swing down and up through the next two beads in the previous row. Make the turn at the other end of the row the same way [**fig. 3, b–c**].

7. Continue working in herringbone stitch as in steps 5 and 6 until the bracelet is about ½ in. (1.3 cm) short of the desired finished length. If you start to run out of thread, end the thread by sewing through the beadwork following the established thread path and tying a few half-hitch knots, making sure you stitch back and forth across at least two or three rows. Add a new thread a few rows below where you left off, and sew through the beadwork following the established pattern, tying a few half-hitch knots between the beads.

8. To add the clasp, sew through the beadwork to exit an outside stack of color-B 8ºs [**fig. 4, a–b**]. Pick up three 15ºs, the first loop on one side of the clasp, and three 15º seed beads, and sew back through the 8º your thread exited to make a loop [**fig. 4, b–c**]. Sew through the beadwork to exit one of the two middle color-A 8ºs, and pick up three 15º seed beads, a center loop on the clasp, and three 15ºs. Sew back through the

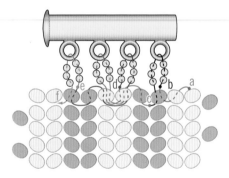

fig. 4

8º your thread exited, and exit the other center color-A 8º [**fig. 4, c–d**]. Attach the other center loop on the clasp the same way, and sew through the beads to exit the remaining outer stack of color-B 8ºs [**fig. 4, d–e**]. Attach the last loop as you did the first [**fig. 4, e–f**]. Sew through the beadwork to go through all the loops again, and end the thread as in step 7.

9. Remove the stop bead, and thread a needle on the tail. Repeat step 8 to attach the other half of the clasp, and end the thread.

TIP

To make sure your clasp is attached so the two parts are aligned properly, close the clasp while you attach the second half.

Just a slight variation in bead shape and size can change the profile of a herringbone strip, adding dimension to bracelets or necklaces.

This bracelet uses 8º and 6º seed beads. The initial ladder uses three 8ºs, four 6ºs, and three 8ºs, and the bracelet is stitched following this pattern with very tight tension.

After a few rows, you'll see that the middle of the bracelet bows up and out, giving the bracelet a distinct curve. Since the curve takes shape only after you've stitched a few more rows (the last few rows you stitched will be floppy), you'll want to add a little extra length and weave back through the last few rows, pulling the tension very tight before attaching the clasp.

PROJECT12
Tubular herringbone necklace

Finished length: 17 in. (43 cm)

MATERIALS & TOOLS

- 2 8 mm accent beads
- 10 g 8° seed beads
- toggle clasp
- nylon beading thread, size D
- beading needle, #12
- scissors or thread snips

Materials note
You can finish this necklace without the accent beads, but they add a polished touch to the ends.

This simple rope, made of two stitches per round, has a boxy shape that looks great in a variety of colors and using all sorts of beads. Tubular herringbone works up fast and can be stiff or slinky depending on your tension. You want the stitches to be tight enough so you don't have gaps between the beads, but loose enough so the strand can move a little.

1. Cut a comfortable length of thread and thread a needle on one end. Attach a stop bead to the other end, leaving a 10-in. (25 cm) tail.

2. Pick up two 8° seed beads, and sew through them both again so they sit side by side. Pick up another 8°, and sew through the previous 8° and the new 8°. Repeat once more for a ladder of four beads [**fig. 1**].

fig. 1

Join the ladder into a ring by sewing through the first 8° and the last 8° once more [**fig. 2**].

fig. 2

3. Pick up two 8°s, and sew down through the next 8° in the previous round [**fig. 3, a–b**]. Sew up through the following 8°, pick up two 8°s, and sew down through the next 8° in the previous round [**fig. 3, b–c**].

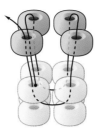

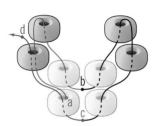

fig. 3

Next, you'll do what's called a **step-up**: Step up to start the next round by sewing through the top two beads in the first column [**fig. 3, c–d**].

4. Continue stitching in tubular herringbone as in step 3 [**fig. 4**], picking up two beads in each stitch and stepping up after each round, until the rope is the desired length. If you start to run out of thread, end the current thread

TIP If you have trouble remembering where to step up, look at the threads between the beads. After the first row you should see uniform thread bridges between each pair of beads in the round.

fig. 4

by sewing through the beads following the herringbone stitch thread path and tying a few half-hitch knots between beads. Add a new thread a few rounds below where you left off, and follow the established thread path, tying a few half-hitch knots between beads, until you exit where you left off.

5. To attach the clasp, pick up the 8 mm accent bead and the loop half of the clasp. Sew back through the 8 mm and the next 8° in the round [**fig. 5, a–b**]. Sew up through the next 8° in the round and sew through the 8 mm and clasp loop again [**fig. 5, a–b**]. Sew back through the 8 mm

and the next 8° in the round [**fig. 5, c–d**]. Sew through the beads again to reinforce the connection, keeping the thread loose enough so the clasp can move. End the thread.

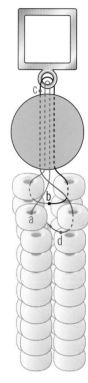

fig. 5

6. Remove the stop bead, and thread a needle on the tail. Repeat step 5 to attach the other half of the clasp.

ANOTHER IDEA

You can make a tubular herringbone strand using any number of beads in the base—as long as it's an even number. Try starting with a ladder of six or eight beads (this bracelet uses eight). You can even try alternating colors or types of beads.

PROJECT 13

Twisted tubular herringbone bangle

It's very easy to give tubular herringbone a little twist, and using two colors of beads creates an endless spiral around your wrist. For this project, you'll start with a loose ring instead of a ladder. When the bracelet is the desired length, you'll pull out the first two rounds and join the ends into a seamless bangle.

Finished circumference: 9 in. (23 cm)

MATERIALS & TOOLS

- 5 g 8º Japanese seed beads, color A
- 5 g 8º Japanese seed beads, color B
- nylon beading thread, size D
- beading needles, #12
- scissors or thread snips

Materials note
In this project, the type of beads you choose makes a big difference. Japanese seed beads work best because they are regular in size and shape. If the beads are irregular, as Czech-made beads tend to be, the irregularity shows in the pattern and makes your stitching look uneven.

TIP

Stitching six 8º seed beads per round is great for a bangle because the resulting rope is sturdy enough to hold its shape when you form it into a circle. Try playing with bead sizes and with your tension. You might find that tiny 15º seed beads make perfect hoop earrings, or that you can make a slinky necklace using eight 11ºs in a round.

1. Cut a comfortable length of thread, and thread a needle on one end. Attach a stop bead to the other, leaving a 10-in. (25 cm) tail.

2. Pick up this pattern three times for a total of six beads: a color-A 8º seed bead and a color-B 8º seed bead. Sew through the first color-A 8º so that the beads form a loose ring [**fig. 1**].

fig. 1

3. Pick up a color-A 8º and a color-B 8º, and sew through the next color-B 8º and color-A 8º in the ring [**fig. 2, a–b**]. Repeat twice to complete the round [**fig. 2, b–c**].

Sew through the first color-A 8º added to step up into position to start the next round [**fig. 2, c–d**].

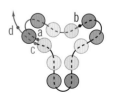

fig. 2

4. Work another round of tubular herringbone as in step 3. When you complete the round, sew up through the top two color-A 8ºs in the first stack of beads to step up to start the next round. Pull the beads tight so they start to form a tube.

5. Now you'll start to add the twist to the stitch. Pick up a color-A 8º and a color-B 8º, and sew down through the next color-B 8º. Instead up sewing up through the top color-A 8º in the next stack, sew up through the top two color-A 8ºs in the next stack [**fig. 3, a–b**].

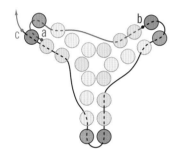

fig. 3

Repeat once for the next stitch, and then work the last stitch of the round. To get into position to start the next round, you'll need to step up by sewing through the top three color-A 8ºs in the first stack [**fig. 3, b–c**].

6. Keep stitching in twisted tubular herringbone until the rope can fit around the widest part of your hand. (You won't see the twist until you've stitched a few rows.) Stitch two or three extra rows.

Pull the thread tight as you stitch, so the tube will be tight enough to hold the bangle shape. Remember, you'll sew down through one bead to finish the stitch and sew up through two beads to start the next one. Don't forget to step up through three beads to start each new round. If you start to run out of thread, end the thread by sewing back through a few rows of beads, following the thread path, and tying a few half-hitch knots between the beads. To add a new thread, sew into the beadwork a few rounds below where you started, and sew through the beads, following the existing thread path and tying a few half-hitch knots between beads. Exit the beadwork where you left off.

7. Remove the stop bead from the tail, and carefully pull out the first two to four rounds of stitching. You want to be able to see a clear pattern of paired beads [**A**]. Make sure your thread is exiting the end of a stack of beads.

8. Using the tail, stitch a round of twisted tubular herringbone following the color pattern (a color-B 8º and a color-A 8º in each stitch). Step up to start the next round.

9. Bring the ends of the bracelet together so that the colors align. You'll see that the gaps between the stitches on each end don't line up [**B**].

10. Using the tail thread, sew into an 8º on the other side the same color as the 8º your thread is exiting. Sew through the next 8º on that end, and then sew through the next 8º on the tail end of the bracelet [**C**].

Think of this as making a twisted herringbone stitch, but instead of adding new beads, you're sewing through the beads on the other end. Sew up through the top two beads in the next stack, and sew between the next pair of matching end beads. Repeat once more.

11. You may see that your join looks a little loose or uneven at this point. Just keep sewing through the beadwork, following the twisted herringbone thread path. You should notice that your thread path duplicates the thread path on the other end.

When you start to run out of tail thread, end the thread. Using the working thread, sew through the beadwork following the existing thread path and tying a few half-hitch knots. If you have some problem spots where the thread is showing, sew through the gap, and pull the thread tight. After the bracelet is securely joined, end the thread.

A

B

C

PROJECT 14
Brick stitch earrings

Brick stitch arranges the beads so they look like classic brickwork—the "seams" between the beads are centered on the beads above and below. Brick stitch has a natural decrease along either side, so it's really easy to create stepped patterns, such as triangles or diamonds. These earrings are a traditional application of the stitch.

MATERIALS & TOOLS

- 2 g 11° seed beads or cylinder beads
- 1 g 15° or 11° seed beads
- pair of earring findings
- nylon beading thread, size D
- beading needles, #12
- chainnose pliers (optional)
- scissors or thread snips

Materials note

Brick stitch allows a lot of flexibility in bead choice. Because you're attaching the beads in layers, you can create very neatly structured beadwork, even when you vary the shapes and sizes of the beads.

If you want your earrings to lie flat, use the same type of bead for the center and the edge of the earrings. If you want the center to pop out, use a slightly smaller bead for the edging than the center.

1. Cut a 1-yd. (.9 m) length of thread, thread a needle on one end, and attach a stop bead in the center of the thread. You'll use the long tail later to work the second half of the earring. You may want to wind the tail on a bobbin or piece of cardboard to keep it out of your way as you work the first half.

2. Pick up a 15° seed bead (this will be the edge bead) and an 11° seed bead (this will be one of the middle beads), and sew through both again so that they sit side by side. Pick up another 11°, and sew through the previous 11° and the new 11° so they sit side by side. Keep working in ladder stitch until your strip has five 11°s with one 15° at each end [**fig. 1**]. If necessary, sew back through the strip so the beads sit straight and tightly together.

fig. 1

3. Look closely at the strip you've stitched, and find the threads that run between the holes of the beads. These are called **thread bridges**. With your thread exiting up out of a 15º, pick up a 15º and an 11º. Slide them down the thread so they are close to the beadwork. Skip the first thread bridge in the previous row (the bridge between the 15º and the 11º), and sew under the next thread bridge and back up through the 11º [**fig. 2, a–b**]. Sew down through the 15º and up through the 11º, pulling the beads tight and snug to the beadwork [**fig. 2, b–c**]. This is the first stitch of the row. The other stitches are different.

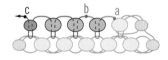

fig. 2

4. Pick up an 11º, and sew under the next thread bridge. Sew back up through the 11º [**fig. 3, a–b**]. Repeat across the row, but when there is just one thread bridge left, pick up a 15º instead of an 11º [**fig. 3, b–c**]. You'll notice that this row is one bead shorter than the first row, making the edges stepped. The edge beads on each side should always be 15ºs.

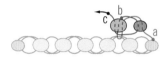

fig. 3

5. Keep working in brick stitch as in steps 3 and 4 for three more rows, ending with a three-bead row. For the next row, work only one stitch, using two 15ºs [**fig. 4**].

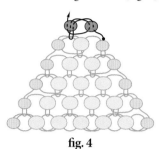

fig. 4

6. For the last stitch, pick up a single 15º, and sew down through the next 15º in the previous row. Sew through the three 15ºs again [**fig. 5**]. End the thread by sewing through the beadwork, and tying a few half-hitch knots between the beads. Trim the thread close to the beadwork.

fig. 5

7. Flip the beadwork over, remove the stop bead, and thread a needle on the tail.

8. Work steps 3–5 on the other side of the beadwork.

9. Add the last bead of the diamond as in step 6, but don't end the thread. Instead, pick up five 15ºs, and sew through the last 15º again to make a loop [**fig. 6**]. Sew through the beads again, and end the thread as in step 6.

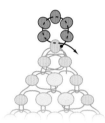

fig. 6

10. Repeat steps 1–9 to make another earring. Attach both earrings to the earring findings, using chainnose pliers to open and close the loops, if necessary.

ANOTHER IDEA

Instead of a simple outline, try adding a pattern to your earrings. You can sketch out the pattern to help you know which beads to pick up, but it's not necessary.

As you stitch, just eliminate the center bead (or one of the center beads, if there are two) from the pattern of the previous row, keeping the pattern symmetrical.

PROJECT 15
Brick stitch bracelet

A wonderful characteristic of brick stitch is that it is so easy to increase and decrease the number of stitches in each row. This means you can stagger the ends of the rows to make a rectangular shape instead of a triangle or diamond, and you can work with different types and sizes of beads without needing elaborate instructions. This bracelet pairs precisely shaped hex-cut cylinder beads with slightly irregular Czech seed beads for a chunky cuff with a channel of texture in the middle.

Finished length: 7 in. (18 cm)

MATERIALS & TOOLS

- 5 g 11º cylinder beads or hex-cut cylinder beads
- 10 g 8º seed beads
- three-strand tube clasp
- 6–8 lb. test GSP thread or nylon beading thread, size D, and thread conditioner
- beading needles, #12
- scissors or thread snips

Materials note
You can combine just about any type and size of bead here. To keep the edges of the bracelet neat and straight, it's best to use a cylinder, hex-cut, or cube bead. As you stitch a project this size, the thread undergoes a lot of wear; conditioning your thread before you start stitching will help avoid tangles (see p. 16).

TIP

In brick stitch, you don't need to follow the existing thread path to hide the thread as you end it and add it; simply sew through the beads on a diagonal. As always, be careful not to pull too tightly, or you'll change the tension of the beadwork.

1. Cut a comfortable length of thread and thread a needle on one end. Attach a stop bead 6 in. (15 cm) from the other end.

2. Pick up two cylinder beads, and sew through them both again so they sit side by side. Pick up another cylinder, and sew through the previous cylinder and the new cylinder so they sit side by side. Repeat to keep working in ladder stitch until your strip is ½ in. (1.3 cm) short of the desired finished length of the bracelet. If necessary, sew back through the strip so that the beads are straight and the beadwork is tight.

3. Find the thread bridges between the beads in the first row. With your thread exiting an end cylinder, pick up two cylinders. Slide them down the thread so they are close to the beadwork. Sew under the thread bridge between the first and second bead in the first row, then sew back through the last cylinder added [**fig. 1, a–b**]. Sew through the first bead and the second bead in the new row again [**fig. 1, b–c**].

fig. 1

Because you sewed under the first thread bridge instead of the second, you just made an increase at the beginning of this row. You'll do this at the start of every row.

4. Pick up a cylinder, sew under the next thread bridge, and sew back up through the new cylinder [**fig. 1, c–d**]. Keep working in brick stitch across the row. On the other end, you'll see that this edge is half a bead shorter than the first row. Every other row will be staggered like this, on both ends of the bracelet.

5. Repeat step 3, but pick up two 8° seed beads instead of two cylinders [**fig. 2, a–b**].

6. To complete the first row of 8°s, work in regular brick stitch. Whenever the beads are too crowded to sew under the next thread bridge, skip that bridge and sew under the next one instead [**fig. 2, b–c**]. The goal is to keep the beads flat and even.

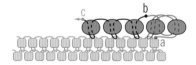

fig. 2

7. Continue working in brick stitch until you've completed seven rows of 8°s. You will not need to skip thread bridges after the first row. You may notice a curve after the first or second row of 8°s, but if you work the remaining rows tightly, it will disappear after a few rows. If you start to run out of thread, end the working thread by sewing through the beadwork and tying a few half-hitch knots between beads. Add the new thread a few rows below where you left off, and sew through the beadwork, tying half-hitch knots between beads, until you reach the point where you left off.

8. To stitch the other edge of the bracelet, you'll switch back to stitching with cylinders, and increase the number of beads in each row. If you want to be precise, you can count the number of cylinders in the first row and match it on the other edge, but it's not necessary to be completely symmetrical.

Pick up two cylinders, and start your row with an increase as in step 3 [**fig. 3, a–b**]. Work across the row in brick stitch. If you find that stitching under the next thread bridge would leave a gap in the beadwork, sew under the same thread bridge you attached the previous stitch to a second time [**fig. 3, b–c**].

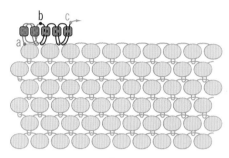

fig. 3

9. Work one more row of brick stitch with cylinder beads. You will not need to attach two stitches to any thread bridges in this row.

10. Look at the ends of your bracelet, where the beadwork is staggered. You'll see that the beads in every other row stick up. These are known as **up-beads**. Sew through the beadwork to exit the first 8° up-bead at the end. Pick up seven 11° seed beads and the first loop on the clasp. Sew back through the first 11° to make a loop, and sew through the next 8° up-bead. Repeat to attach the other loops between up-beads [**A**]. Retrace your thread path through the loops again for added security.

11. Add a new thread to the other end of the bracelet, and repeat step 10 to attach the other half of the clasp to the bracelet. Make sure the clasp ends are lined up correctly so the clasp will close. End all the threads.

A

PROJECT16
Circular brick stitch pendant

You don't need to start brick stitch with a ladder. As long as you have a thread or wire to sew under in the first row, you can work brick stitch. Because it's so easy to create increases, brick stitch is well suited to working in the round. This pendant uses a round bead in the center. Increases in each row create a flat, circular frame. Add a trim of crystal fringe for a sunburst effect.

Diameter: 1⅛ in. (2.9 cm)

MATERIALS & TOOLS

- 10 mm round bead, such as a faux pearl
- 16 3 mm crystals
- 3 g 15º Charlotte seed beads
- nylon beading thread, size D
- beading needles, #12 or #13
- scissors or thread snips

Materials note

Charlottes have a somewhat squat shape that I like for circular brick stitch; their shape makes it easy to increase as you stitch the first row, and their tiny facets create a fine, detailed pattern.

If you find the beads too small to work with comfortably, regular 15ºs will work just as well.

TIP

Stitch up two of these components for a great pair of large earrings, or string three or more as dangles on a necklace.

1. Cut a 1-yd. (.9 m) length of thread, thread a needle on one end, and pick up the 10 mm bead, leaving a 6 in. (15 cm) tail.

2. Pick up enough 15º Charlotte seed beads to span one half of the circumference of the 10 mm, and sew through the 10 mm again [**fig. 1, a–b**]. Pick up enough 15ºs to span the other half of the 10 mm, and sew through the 10 mm again [**fig. 1, b–c**]. Sew through all the 15ºs to make a ring with no gaps [**fig. 1, c–d**]. End the tail by sewing through the 15ºs and tying half-hitch knots around the thread. Sew through the 10 mm at least once more, and trim the tail.

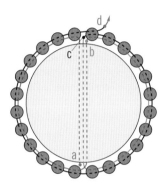

fig. 1

3. Pick up two 15ºs, and slide them down the thread so they are close to the initial ring. Sew under the thread between two of the beads in the ring, and back up through the second 15º just added. Pick up a 15º, and sew under the thread between the next two beads in the ring and back through the 15º just added [**fig. 2**].

fig. 2

4. Continue around in brick stitch, skipping beads in the initial ring or sewing under the thread bridge for two stitches as needed to make a smooth circle. To finish the round, exit the last bead added, and sew through the first 15º picked up in the round, under the thread between the beads in the ring, and back through the first 15º [**fig. 3**].

5. Work a second round of brick stitch off of the first, increasing by attaching two stitches to a thread bridge when necessary. The goal is to keep the circle of beads flat. Step up to start the new round as in step 4.

fig. 3

6. To add the crystal fringe, pick up a 15º, and sew under the next thread bridge. Pick up a 3 mm crystal round and three 15ºs, and sew back through the 3 mm and under the next thread bridge [**fig. 4**]. Repeat around the circle, skipping thread bridges as needed. For the last 3 mm stitch, pick up enough 15ºs to make a loop that will accommodate a jump ring, chain, or cord (usually at least seven). End the thread.

fig. 4

PROJECT**17**
Spiral rope bracelet

This easy spiraling stitch is great for creating loose, fringy ropes for bracelets and necklaces. As you stitch, you'll create loops that revolve around a core of seed beads. You can make the loops larger if you like—they just need to fit around the core beads as you make each stitch.

Finished length: 8 in. (20 cm)

MATERIALS & TOOLS

- 3 g 8º seed beads
- 5 g 4 mm drop beads, 3 mm magatamas, or 8º seed beads in a different color
- lobster claw clasp with soldered jump ring, tag, or split ring
- nylon beading thread, size D
- beading needles, #10 or #12
- scissors or thread snips

Materials note
I like the bubbly texture that drops and magatamas add to the outer spiral, but regular seed beads are lovely on their own. Using two colors helps the spiral stand out and makes it easy to keep track of stitches.

A

1. Cut a 2-yd. (1.8 m) length of thread and thread a needle on one end. Attach a stop bead to the other end, leaving an 8-in. (20 cm) tail.

2. Pick up two 8º seed beads (the **core beads**) and three drops, magatamas, or color-B 8º seed beads, and sew through the two 8ºs again to make a loop. Flip the drops (the **loop beads**) to the left of the core beads [**A**].

TIP The loops in spiral rope often shift, making it hard to see the spiral pattern. Usually, simply twisting the rope until the loops cluster into a spiral before wearing will fix this problem. But keep an eye on your work as you stitch: If you see a lot of thread between your core beads, your tension is too loose. Don't end the thread. Instead, keep working until the rope is about 1 in. (2.5 cm) longer than the desired finished length. Attach the first half of the clasp, and sew back through all the core beads, pulling the thread tight to close the gaps. At the other end, attach other half of the clasp, and end the thread.

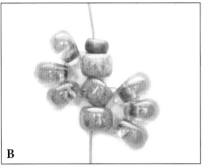

B

3. Pick up an 8º and three drops, and sew through the last 8º and the 8º you just picked up [**B**]. Pull tight, and flip the drops to the left, on top of the first three drops. If it's more comfortable for you to flip the loops of drops to the right, you can—just make sure you flip the loop to the same side in every stitch.

4. Keep working in spiral rope by picking up an 8º and three drops, and sewing through the last 8º in the previous stitch and the 8º just added. Flip the loops to the same side in every stitch. Make sure you pull each stitch tight, so that the 8ºs are tightly stacked with no gaps—your loop beads shouldn't slip between the core beads. Work until the rope is ½ in. (1.3 cm) short of the desired length.

5. Using the working thread, pick up the loop on the lobster claw clasp, and sew back through the last two 8ºs. Sew through the loop of drops and the last three 8ºs. Sew through the next loop of drops, and then out the end 8º. Sew through the loop of the lobster claw clasp again. Repeat until the clasp is secure, and then end the thread by sewing through a few loops and tying half-hitch knots between the beads.

6. On the other end of the bracelet, remove the stop bead, and attach a needle. Repeat step 5 using the tail and the tag, soldered jump ring, or split ring.

ANOTHER IDEA

You're not limited to two types of beads in a spiral rope. You can use a mixture of beads for all the loops. I like to create longer loops of beads in the middle of the necklace and smaller loops at the ends, so the necklace is fuller in the front.

For this necklace variation, I used three sizes of fire-polished beads (3 mm, 5 mm, and 8 mm) and two sizes of seed beads (11ºs and 8ºs), and did a little planning: I left a long tail, in case I needed to add length, then I worked a few stitches with just seed beads, using 8º seed beads for the core and 11º seed beads for the loops. Then I worked in spiral rope using two 11ºs, a 3 mm fire polished bead, and two 11ºs until I'd used half of the 3 mms. I did the same thing with the 5 mm fire-polished beads. Then I stitched the middle of the necklace using all of my 8 mm fire-polished beads. I finished by using the rest of the 5 mms, then the 3 mms, and finally worked a few stitches with seed beads. Depending on the beads you use, you'll need to adjust the number of seed beads in each loop so that the loops look even and round.

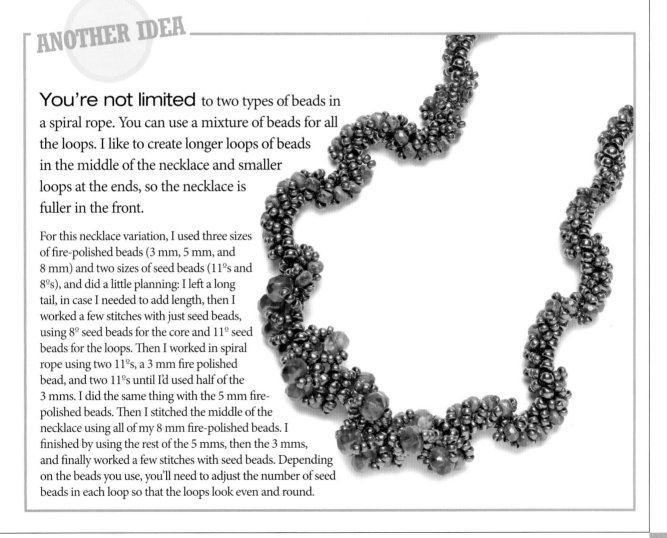

PROJECT18
Flat spiral bracelet

It's easy to create a flat band with looped edges by alternating the direction of the loops as you finish each stitch. I like to alternate the colors of the loops to give the edges a striped look.

Finished length: 6½ in. (16.5 cm)

MATERIALS & TOOLS

- 4 g 6º seed beads
- 3 g 8º seed beads, color A
- 3 g 8º seed beads, color B
- lobster claw clasp and soldered jump ring, tag, or split ring
- nylon beading thread, size D
- beading needles, #10 or #12
- scissors or thread snips

Materials note
Larger seed beads like 8º s make denser loops along the edges. If you use smaller beads, like 11º s, the loops will be more open and lacy.

A

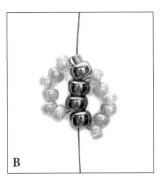

B

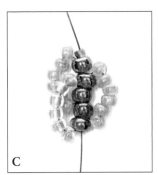

C

D

1. Cut a 2-yd. (1.8 m) length of thread, and thread a needle on one end. Attach a stop bead to the other end, leaving an 8-in. (20 cm) tail.

2. Pick up three 6º seed beads and six color A 8º seed beads, and sew through the three 6ºs again to make a loop. Flip the loop to the left of the core beads [**A**].

3. Pick up a 6º and six color-A 8ºs, and sew through the last two 6ºs in the previous stitch and the 6º you just picked up. Pull tight, and flip the loop to the right [**B**].

4. Pick up a 6º and six color-B 8ºs, and sew through the last two 6ºs in the previous stitch and the 6º just added. Pull tight and flip the loop to the left [**C**].

Repeat, this time flipping the loop to the right [**D**].

5. Keep working in flat spiral rope as in step 4, but alternate the colors of the 8ºs so you work two stitches with color-A 8ºs, then two stitches with color-B 8ºs. Stitch until the rope is ½ in. (1.3 cm) short of the desired length.

6. Using the working thread, pick up the loop on the lobster claw clasp, and sew back through the last three 6ºs. Sew through the loops of 8ºs, and through the loop on the clasp several times, then end the thread by tying a few half-hitch knots between beads.

7. On the other end of the bracelet, remove the stop bead, and thread a needle. Repeat step 6 using the tail and the tag, soldered jump ring, or split ring.

TIP I used a fairly large lobster claw clasp for this bracelet. If yours is smaller, you may need to add a few stitches to make sure your bracelet fits comfortably. When you wrap your bracelet around your wrist to test the length, compare the gap between the ends to the size of your clasp and jump ring or tag, and keep in mind how loose a fit you'd like.

PROJECT 19
Double spiral rope necklace

Finished length: 16 in. (41 cm)

MATERIALS & TOOLS

- 10 g 6° seed beads
- 12 g 8° seed beads
- 10 g 11° seed beads
- toggle clasp
- nylon beading thread, size D
- beading needles, #12
- scissors or thread snips

Materials note
You can use all 8°s or all 11°s for both sets of loops in this necklace, but I like the texture that using both sizes of beads adds to the spirals.

Double spiral rope is denser than regular spiral rope, and the spiralling pattern is much more defined. It can be a little harder to stitch the second spiral than the first, but if you keep the first rope twisted so the spiral pattern is easy to see, you'll have no problem.

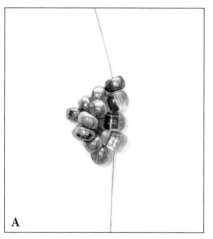

A

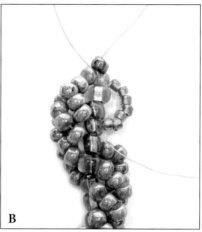

B

C

1. Cut a 2-yd. (1.8 m) length of thread, and thread a needle on one end. Attach a stop bead to the other end, leaving an 8-in. (20 cm) tail.

2. Pick up two 6º seed beads and five 8º seed beads, and sew through the two 6ºs again to make a loop. Flip the loop of 8ºs to the left.

3. Pick up a 6º and five 8ºs, and sew through the last 6º and the 6º you just picked up. Pull tight, and flip the loop to the left, placing it on top of the first loop [**A**]. Repeat until the necklace is about 1 in. (2.5 cm) short of the desired finished length. Attach a stop bead to the end of the necklace to hold the stitches in place as you work the second spiral. Twist the rope so the spiral is clearly defined.

4. Cut a new 2-yd. (1.8 m) length of thread, thread a needle, and attach a stop bead, leaving an 8-in. (20 cm) tail. Sew through the two end 6ºs, exiting the core beads so that the 8º spirals are out of the way. Pick up seven 11º seed beads, and sew through the last two 6ºs and the next 6º [**B**].

5. Look carefully at the rope. Find the end loop of 8ºs and take note of which side it is on. You'll want to flip your new loops the other way. So if your end loop of 8ºs is on the left, you'll flip your 11ºs to the right. Pick up seven 11ºs, and sew through the last two 6ºs that your thread passed through and the next 6º. Flip the 11ºs to the same side as the last loop [**C**].

6. Keep stitching in spiral rope to add loops of 11ºs until you reach the other end of the necklace. Make sure you exit the core beads on the same side of the existing 8º loops every time.

7. Using the working thread, pick up five 11ºs, the loop on the toggle clasp, and five 11ºs. Sew back through the last two 6ºs and the loops of 11ºs. Sew through the 6ºs, loops, and clasp loop a few more times, then end the thread by tying a few half-hitch knots between beads. Remove the stop bead on the other thread, and end the thread.

8. Remove one of the stop beads at the other end of the necklace, thread a needle, and repeat step 7 to attach the other half of the toggle clasp. End both threads.

It can be easier to maneuver a toggle clasp if the ends of the necklace are thinner than the rest of it. I worked a few stitches just using 6ºs and 11ºs to taper the ends a little.

PROJECT20
Netted cuff bracelet

Netting can be worked in many different ways. You can make the spaces between the beads as large as you'd like—just pick up a different number of beads in each stitch. This bracelet uses the natural stretch of netting to make a seamless cuff. Stretch it to fit over the wide part of your hand, and it will snug up once it's around your wrist.

Finished length: 6 in. (15 cm)

MATERIALS & TOOLS

- 10 g 11º cylinder beads
- 4 g 11º seed beads
- GSP thread, 6 lb. test
- beading needles, #12
- scissors or thread snips

Materials note
Because this bracelet needs to stretch to fit around your hand, the thread undergoes a bit more stress than normal. Using GSP thread will help you avoid broken threads.

1. Cut a comfortable length of thread, and thread a needle on one end. Attach a stop bead to the other end, leaving a 6-in. (15 cm) tail.

2. Pick up a pattern of an 11° seed bead and two cylinder beads ten times for a total of 30 beads. Skip the last 11 beads, and sew back through the next bead, an 11° seed bead [**fig. 1, a–b**]. A symmetrical loop will form.

3. Pick up two cylinders, an 11°, and two cylinders, skip the next five beads, and sew through the next bead, an 11° [**fig. 1, b–c**]. Repeat to the end of the row [**fig. 1, c–d**].

4. To make the turn and start the next row, pick up two cylinders and an 11° twice, then pick up two cylinders for a total of eight beads. Skip the last 11° in the previous row, and sew through the next 11°, the center 11° in the next stitch [**fig. 2, a–b**].

5. Repeat steps 3 and 4 [**fig. 2, b–c**] until the bracelet fits around your wrist. Notice that with each stitch, you sew through the center 11° of the next stitch in the previous row. If you start to run out of thread, end the thread by sewing back through the beadwork, following the established thread path, and tying half-hitch knots around the thread between the beads. Add a new thread by sewing into the beadwork a few rows below where you left off, and sewing through the beads, tying half-hitch knots between the beads, until you exit the beadwork where you left off.

6. Make sure the bracelet will fit around the widest part of your hand. If it doesn't, stitch a few more rows.

7. Align the ends. You want the two end rows to match, so the outer 11°s on one end line up with the inner 11°s on the other. Stitch the final row by picking up cylinders and sewing through the center 11°s in each stitch on the other end of the bracelet [**fig. 3**]. End the thread and the tail.

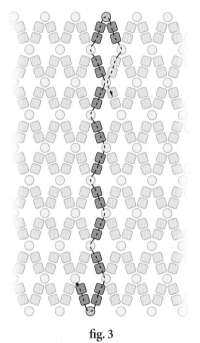

fig. 3

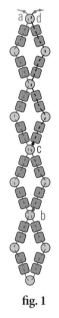

fig. 1

fig. 2

You can use just about any type of bead in netting, but when you're learning, it's easier to find the bead you'll sew through if it's a different color or shape than the other beads. In my bracelet, the beads are close in color but the finish and shape distinguish them a bit.

PROJECT 21
Tubular netted necklace

Finished length: 15 in. (38 cm)

MATERIALS & TOOLS

- 8 g 15° seed beads
- clasp
- GSP thread, 6 lb. test
- beading needles, #12
- scissors or thread snips

Materials note
I chose 15° seed beads for this
project to make a dainty, thin rope,
but you can use any size seed
beads to make this rope.

The only difficult part of tubular
netting is figuring out how many beads to
pick up for the first stitch (often three, five,
or seven beads). This necklace is a simple
hollow tube that is thin and cord-like—
the perfect setting for a pendant
or special bead.

1. Cut a comfortable length of thread, and thread a needle on one end. Attach a stop bead to the other end, leaving a 6-in. (15 cm) tail.

2. Pick up 12 15º seed beads, and sew through the first three beads again to form a ring [**fig. 1, a–b**]. You may find it helpful to place the ring on a toothpick and work around it for the first few rounds.

3. Pick up three 15ºs, skip three 15ºs in the ring, and sew through the next 15º [**fig. 1, b–c**]. Repeat twice [**fig. 1, c–d**], and sew through the first two beads added this round to step up [**fig. 1, d–e**].

4. To continue in tubular netting, pick up three beads, skip three beads, and sew through the next bead [**fig. 2, a–b**]. Repeat twice, [**fig. 2, b–c**] and step up to start the next round by sewing through the first two 15ºs of the new round [**A**]. Repeat this step to stitch until your tube is ½ in. (1.3 cm) short of your desired finished length.

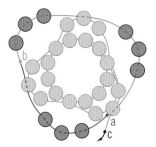

fig. 2

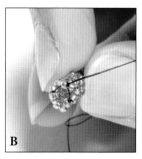

A

B

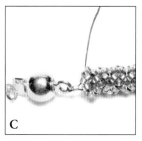

C

If you start to run out of thread, end the thread by sewing back through a few rounds and tying half-hitch knots between beads. Add a new thread by sewing into the beadwork a few rows before where you left off, and tying a few half-hitch knots between beads. Exit where you left off.

5. To end the necklace, exit the center bead in the first stitch of the last round. Sew through the center bead in each stitch of the last round, and pull the thread tight to

draw them together [**B**]. Pick up a 15º and a loop of the clasp, and sew back through the 15º [**C**]. Sew through the next bead in the last round, and sew through the 15º and the loop of the clasp again. Repeat one last time, and end the thread.

6. Remove the stop bead from the other end of the necklace, attach a needle, and repeat step 5 to attach the other half of the clasp and end the thread.

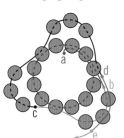

fig. 1

ANOTHER IDEA

Netting is an open and airy stitch that you can see right through. To add a little extra color to your strand, work a netted tube large enough to fit around a simple strand of beads. This bracelet started with a strand of 20 beads and uses five netted beads in each stitch. Before you end the tube, string the large beads on a separate thread, and pull the strand through the tube. End the thread from the strand in the netted tube, and attach the clasp as usual.

PROJECT22
Basic peyote stitch bracelet

Peyote stitch is a versatile stitch, and even-count peyote is the best place to start learning it. Peyote stitch looks similar to brick stitch, but it is worked in a very different way. For each stitch, you'll pick up a new bead, and sew through the next up-bead in the previous row.

Finished length: 7¼ in. (18.4 cm)

MATERIALS & TOOLS

- 3 g 8º cylinder beads, color A
- 3 g 8º cylinder beads, color B
- 1 g 11º seed or cylinder beads
- toggle clasp
- GSP thread, 6 lb. test
- beading needles, #12
- scissors or thread snips

Materials note

Cylinder beads are the best beads to use while learning peyote because of their regular size and squared-off shape. As you work each stitch, each bead will pop into place (sometimes you can even hear it). Cylinder beads are perfect for learning to create pieces with consistent tension.

1. Cut a 1-yd. (.9 m) length of thread, and thread a need on one end. Attach a stop bead to the other end, leaving a 10-in. (25 cm) tail.

2. Pick up a color-A 8° seed bead, two color-B 8° seed beads, and a color-A 8°. These four beads will make up the first two rows of the bracelet.

3. Pick up a color-A 8°, turn, skip the last color-A 8°, and sew through the next bead, a color-B 8° [**fig. 1, a–b**]. Pick up a color-B 8°, skip the next color-B 8°, and sew through the following color-A 8° [**fig. 1, b–c**]. Pull the thread tight to snug up these beads. These are the first three rows. You can count the rows by counting the beads on each end of the band and adding them together; right now your band has one bead on one edge and two beads on the other, so there are three rows.

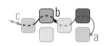

fig. 1

4. Turn, pick up a color-A 8°, and sew through the next up-bead, a color-B 8°. Pick up a color-B 8°, and sew through the next up-bead, an A 8° [**fig. 2**]. Repeat this step until your bracelet is about 1 in. (2.5 cm) short of the desired finished length.

fig. 2

5. Sew through the beads to exit between the two color-B 8°s at one end of the band. Pick up four 11° seed beads or cylinder beads, the loop of half of the clasp, and four 11°s. Sew into the next B 8° [**fig. 3**]. Sew through the beadwork so you can retrace the thread path through the clasp loop several times. End the thread by sewing through the beadwork for a few rows, tying half-hitch knots

between the beads. With peyote stitch, it's important not to pull the thread too tight when sewing through the beads on a diagonal. If you pull too tight, you'll distort the beadwork.

6. Remove the stop bead from the other end of the bracelet, thread a needle on the tail, repeat step 5 to attach the other half of the clasp, and end the tail.

fig. 3

ANOTHER IDEA

This two-drop peyote bracelet is the most-basic variation of an even-count peyote bracelet, but it has a different texture. Instead of picking up one bead in each stitch, you can pick up two beads and treat each pair of beads as though it were a single bead.

For the first two rows of this bracelet, I picked up two color-A 11° cylinders, two color-B 11° cylinders, two color-A cylinders, and two color-B cylinders. Then I turned and picked up two color-B cylinders for the first stitch of the third row.

I worked the rest of the row as though it were regular even-count peyote stitch, picking up two beads for each stitch instead of one.

Peyote stitch locks beads together in

a consistent, regular pattern, making it great for
creating patterns and pictures using different colors
of beads. The beads in peyote stitch make stepped
patterns, perfect for diagonal stripes, diamonds, and
zigzags. This pattern alternates a single diagonal line
with a double line, making the pattern easy to see
from a distance.

Read a peyote stitch **pattern** starting at the bottom. To work
the pattern, pick up all the beads for the first two rows (outlined
in bold), keeping in mind that the first two rows are staggered.
Turn, and pick up the first bead in the third row.

Skip the end bead in the first row, and sew through the next
bead [**figure, a–b**]. Pick up the next bead, skip a bead in the
initial strip, and sew through the next bead. Repeat across the
strip [**figure, b–c**], keeping a close eye on your pattern as you
stitch. Turn, and stitch the next row.

It's very easy for the beads in the first two or three rows to twist
as you stitch, which can distort your pattern, so make sure you
are sewing through the correct up-bead with each stitch.

After you have four or five rows completed, the pattern becomes
much easier to see and the beadwork will no longer twist.

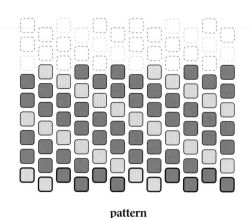

pattern

figure

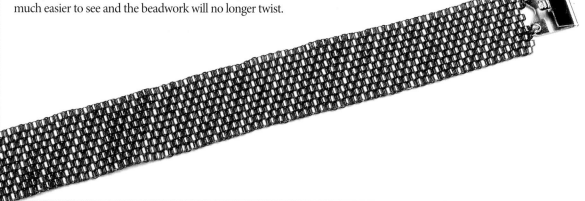

When you have a complicated pattern, a sticky note can be your best
friend: Place the note below each row of the printed pattern to help
you keep track as you stitch. (You'll see the top half of the beads in the
previous row peeking out.)

Peyote patterns usually only show the beads for the first repeat. After
you've worked those rows, start over at the bottom of the pattern.

PROJECT 23
Odd-count peyote bracelet

Odd-count peyote stitch is often used for creating symmetrical designs, as in the chevron pattern of this bracelet. This simple-looking project uses a variety of basic peyote techniques, including a stitched toggle clasp for a seamless finish.

Finished length: 7¼ in. (18.4 cm)

MATERIALS & TOOLS

- 6 g 8° cylinder beads, color A
- 6 g 8° cylinder beads, color B
- GSP thread, 6 lb. test, or nylon beading thread, size D
- beading needles, #12
- scissors or thread snips

Materials note
When working with patterns, try using varied bead finishes along with color contrast to help the pattern stand out. Pair light-colored luster-finish beads with dark matte beads, or dark opaque beads with bright transparent colors.

Because certain colors will pop and others will recede, the contrast will add a lot of dimension to a stitched pattern.

1. Cut a comfortable length of thread, and thread a needle on one end. Attach a stop bead to the other end, leaving a 15-in. (38 cm) tail. You'll use this tail later to stitch or attach part of the clasp (see "Stitch up a peyote toggle clasp," p. 83).

2. Pick up a color-A 8º cylinder, two color-B 8º cylinders, a color-A cylinder, two color-B cylinders, and a color-A cylinder. These beads will make up the first two rows of the bracelet [**pattern** and **fig. 1, a–b**].

3. Turn, pick up a color-B cylinder, skip the last bead in the first row, and sew through the next bead, a color-B cylinder [**fig. 1, b–c**]. Work across the row, following the pattern [**fig. 1, c–d**].

4. When you get to the end of the row, there is no up-bead to sew through, so you'll need to make the first odd-count turn. Think of this turn as a figure 8: Sew through the

pattern

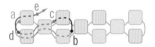

fig. 1

bead directly below the end bead and the following two beads [**fig. 2, a–b**]. Turn, and sew through the bead above it [**fig. 2, b–c**]. Sew through the next bead, then the edge bead in the lower row [**fig. 2, c–d**]. Turn, and sew through the last bead added to the third row [**fig. 2, d–e**]. You are now in position to start the next row.

fig. 2

5. Work across the row in peyote stitch, following the pattern. When you get the end of the row, make the normal, even-count peyote turn [**fig. 3, a–b**]. Work back across the row in peyote stitch [**fig. 3, b–c**]. This time, instead of making the figure-8 odd-count turn, simply sew under the thread bridge between the beads on the edge of the bracelet, and back through the last bead added to the row [**fig. 3, c–d**].

6. Repeat step 5 until the bracelet is 1 in. (2.5 cm) short of the desired finished length. If necessary, end the thread, and add a new thread. Attach a purchased clasp or stitch a clasp as shown on the next page.

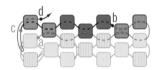

fig. 3

Stitch up a peyote toggle clasp

You can create the perfect stitched toggle bar by working a small strip of peyote and zipping up the ends. To make the loop side of the clasp, work short rows of peyote stitch or a ladder-stitched strip of beads off each side of the bracelet, and connect them at the top.

Toggle bar: peyote stitch zip-up

The toggle bar should be as wide as or wider than your bracelet. This toggle bar is the same width as a bracelet.

Pick up the same number of beads as you did for your bracelet, turn, and begin working in peyote stitch as detailed in the first part of step 3 of the bracelet project **[A]**. Stitch an even number or rows (usually eight, ten, or twelve), depending on the bead size.

Curl the strip into a tube so the ends meet. The up-beads on one end will fit into the gaps on the other end. With your working thread, turn, and sew through the up-beads on each end of the bracelet **[B]**. End the working thread and tail.

If you need to add a row to the end of your bar to make it wider, do not end the thread. Instead, pick up two beads, and sew under the thread bridge between the next two beads on the edge. Sew through the last bead you picked up, pick up a new bead, and sew under the next thread bridge **[C]**. Keep working around the edge in brick stitch, then end by sewing through that first bead and ending the thread.

There are plenty of ways to attach the toggle bar to the bracelet band. You can use a short strand of beads or stitch several together with ladder stitch.

A

B

C

Loop side: peyote short rows

This bracelet uses short rows that extend both edges of the bracelet to create a clasp loop. Following the established color pattern, on one end of the bracelet, turn, pick up a bead, and sew through the next up-bead. Turn, pick up a new bead, and sew through the edge bead. Repeat until there are nine beads in your short rows **[fig. 1]**. Sew through the beadwork, and repeat on the other edge.

Pick up enough beads to span the gap between the short rows (in this case, three), and sew through the top two beads on the other side **[fig. 2, a–b]**. Turn, and sew through the beadwork to exit the same bead you sewed through. Work peyote stitch across the row **[fig. 2, b–c]**, then sew back and forth through the beads several times before ending the thread.

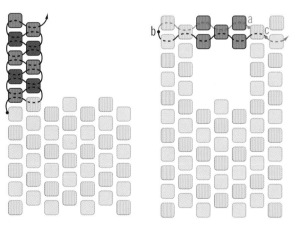

fig. 1   fig. 2

PROJECT24
Tubular peyote stitch necklace

Finished length: 17½ in. (44.5 cm)

MATERIALS & TOOLS

- 2 8 mm round beads
- 10 g 11º seed beads
- clasp
- GSP thread, 6 lb. test, or nylon beading thread, size D
- beading needles, #12
- scissors or thread snips

To make this necklace, you'll work peyote stitch in a circle to form a tube. You may find it helpful to work around a form to start your tube (toothpicks work just fine). After a few rounds, the stitches are well defined, and you'll find yourself flying along.

ANOTHER IDEA

You can add all sorts of stripes and spirals to your tubular peyote pattern. First, determine the type of pattern you'd like to create. This necklace uses a double thickness stripe pattern. It can help to sketch out your pattern before starting.

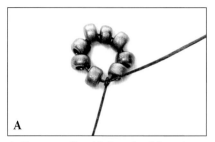

A

B

C

1. Cut a comfortable length of thread, and thread a needle on one end. Attach a stop bead to the other end, leaving a 10-in. (25 cm) tail.

2. Pick up eight 11° seed beads, and tie the working thread and tail together with a square knot, forming a loose ring [**A**]. Sew through the first bead.

3. Pick up a bead, skip the next bead in the ring, and sew through the following bead [**B**]. Repeat around the ring.

4. When you finish the round, you'll need to step up to start the next round: After you pick up the last bead in the

round, skip a bead, sew through the next bead as usual, then sew through the first bead added in the new round [**C**].

5. Continue working in tubular peyote as in steps 3 and 4 until the necklace is about 1 in. (2.5 cm) short of the desired finished length, ending and adding thread as needed.

When adding thread to tubular peyote, it's best to stitch around the tube, rather than turning and reversing direction, which can distort the tension.

6. To attach the clasp, pick up an 8 mm, two to four seed beads, half of

the clasp, and two to four seed beads. Sew back through the 8 mm, and sew through the next up-bead. Retrace the thread path through the 8 mm and clasp loop, and sew through the next up-bead. Repeat around to center and secure the clasp, then end the thread.

7. Repeat step 6 on the other end of the necklace using the tail. Adjust the number of seed beads so the clasp sits comfortably. This necklace uses more seed beads for the toggle bar than the loop so the bar can pivot easily.

ANOTHER IDEA

Odd-count tubular peyote

is very much like regular tubular peyote, but there's no step-up.

Start by picking up an odd number of beads and sewing through the first bead again to make a ring. (This bracelet starts with five beads.) Pick up a bead, skip the next bead, and sew through the following bead.

Keep peyote-stitching around the ring. When you get to the starting point, you'll see that there is no need to step up. You can work the next stitch and sew through the next up-bead. Just keep spiraling!

PROJECT25
Peyote stitch bezel

After you've learned to stitch even-count tubular peyote, it's just one simple step to creating beaded bezels and rings: Change the size of the beads. A bezel is a band or bracket that holds an undrilled component in place. This pendant features a crystal rivoli, which looks terrific in many jewelry projects, including necklaces, earrings, and bracelets.

Diameter: 11/16 in. (1.7 cm)

MATERIALS & TOOLS

- 2 g 11º cylinder beads
- 2 g 15º seed beads
- 14 mm crystal rivoli
- GSP thread, 6 lb. test, or nylon beading thread, size D
- beading needles, #13
- scissors or thread snips

Materials note

Using 11º cylinders and 15ºs is the standard for stitching bezels, but once you're comfortable with the technique, start experimenting. You can use 11º seed beads, Charlottes, even triangles—just find the even number that fits loosely around the outer edge of your stone.

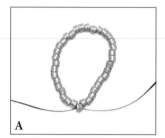

A

1. Cut a 1-yd. (.9 m) length of thread, thread a needle on one end, and attach a stop bead at the midpoint of the thread.

2. Pick up enough 11º cylinder beads to make a loose ring around the rivoli (it must be an even number). I started with 36 cylinders for this 14 mm rivoli. Sew through the first cylinder to form a ring [A].

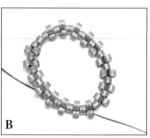

B

3. Work a round of tubular peyote stitch, picking up one cylinder in each stitch. Step up at the end of the round [B].

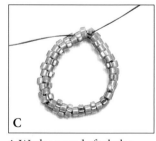

C

4. Work a round of tubular peyote stitch using 15º seed beads, pulling each stitch snug as you work around the ring [C]. You'll see the ring start to cup a little. Step up, and work a second round of tubular peyote stitch using 15ºs.

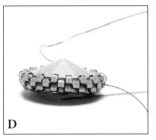

D

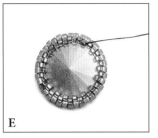

E

F

5. Place the rivoli in the cupped ring [**D**]. I find that the first half of my bezel usually looks a little better than the second half, so I place my rivolis face down in the bezel.

6. Using the tail thread, step up to start a round of tubular peyote stitch on the other side of the initial ring. Work two rounds using 15ºs, pulling the thread tight to secure the ring around the rivoli [**E**].

7. To make a simple loop to hang the rivoli from, end the thread in front by sewing through a few rounds of the beadwork. Sew through the beadwork using the other thread until your thread exits a cylinder in the middle round of beads. Pick up enough 15ºs to make a hanging loop (I used 12 beads). Sew through the cylinder again [**F**]. Sew through the loop of beads again, and end the thread.

ANOTHER IDEA

A peyote-stitched toggle bar with a tubular peyote ring as a clasp is an artful way to finish a necklace. I also love linking rings to make chains. There's so much you can do with peyote-stitched rings, and they are very easy to create after you get a feel for how the size of the beads affects the curve of the tube.

First, follow steps 1–4 of the bezel project using 11º cylinders and 15º seed beads to make a ring that's starting to cup. Stitch one more round using 15ºs, then work three rounds with cylinders. You'll have a ring with two edges curving out with the little 15ºs are in the middle. Work three rounds using 11ºs, and zip up the last round of seed beads with the first round of cylinders.

To make a chain of joined links, simply pass a strand of cylinders through the first ring before joining the strand into a ring. You'll need to rotate the ring a bit as you stitch.

PROJECT26
St. Petersburg chain necklace

Finished length: 16¼ in. (41.3 cm)

MATERIALS & TOOLS

- 10 mm rondelle bead
- 8 g 3 mm magatamas
- 8 g 11° cylinder beads
- nylon beading thread, size D
- beading needle, #12 or #13
- scissors or thread snips

Materials note
If you can't find magatamas, substitute 11° seed beads or fringe drops.

St. Petersburg chain is an asymmetrical stitch that creates a thin, stepped chain. It's perfect for necklaces, lariats, and bracelets. Because you stitch back and forth and in a circle for each stitch, this chain can seem a little overwhelming. Start with cylinder beads, and pull the thread tight after each step, and you'll master the stitch in no time.

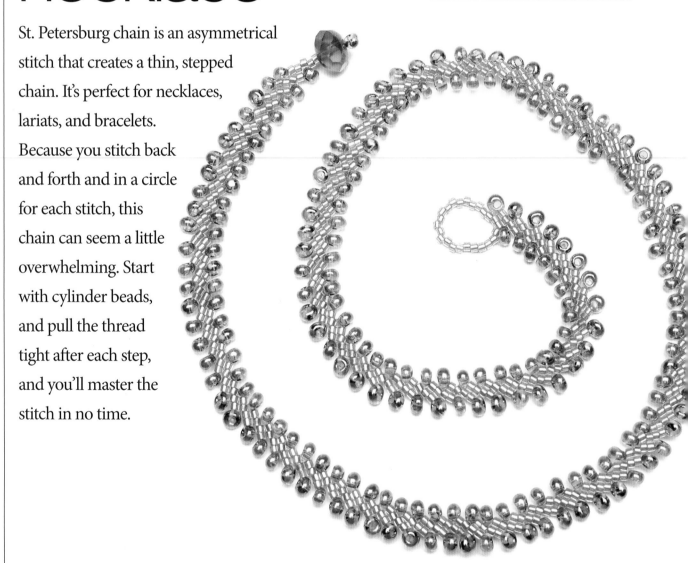

1. Cut a 2-yd. (1.8 m) length of thread, and thread a needle on one end. Attach a stop bead 10 in. (25 cm) from the other end.

2. Pick up six 11º cylinder beads. Sew through the third and fourth cylinders again, so the fifth and sixth cylinders form a second column next to them [**fig. 1**].

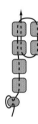

fig. 1

3. Pick up a magatama, and sew back through the next three cylinders in the column [**fig. 2**].

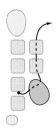

fig. 2

4. Pick up a magatama, and sew through the two cylinders in the next column [**fig. 3**].

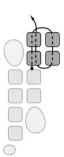

fig. 3

5. Pick up four cylinders, and sew through the first two cylinders just picked up again, sliding the four cylinders tight to the existing chain [**fig. 4**].

fig. 4

6. Pick up a magatama, and sew back through the last three cylinders in the column. Pick up a magatama, and sew through the two cylinders in the next column [**fig. 5**].

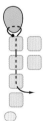

fig. 5

7. Repeat steps 5 and 6 until you are within ½ in. (1.3 cm) of the desired finished length of the necklace.

8. Pick up two cylinders, the 10 mm rondelle, and a magatama. Sew back through the 10 mm and cylinders [**fig. 6**]. Sew through the cylinders in a circle, and sew through the two cylinders, 10 mm, and magatama again. Sew back into the beadwork, and end the thread.

9. Remove the stop bead from the tail, and pick up enough seed beads to make a loop around the 10 mm. Sew through the first column of beads and the loop again, then sew into the beadwork [**fig. 7**]. End the thread.

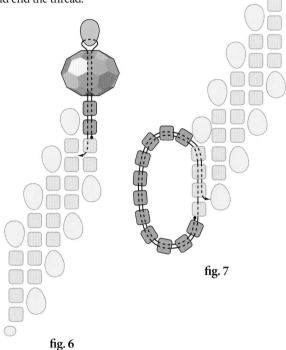

fig. 6

fig. 7

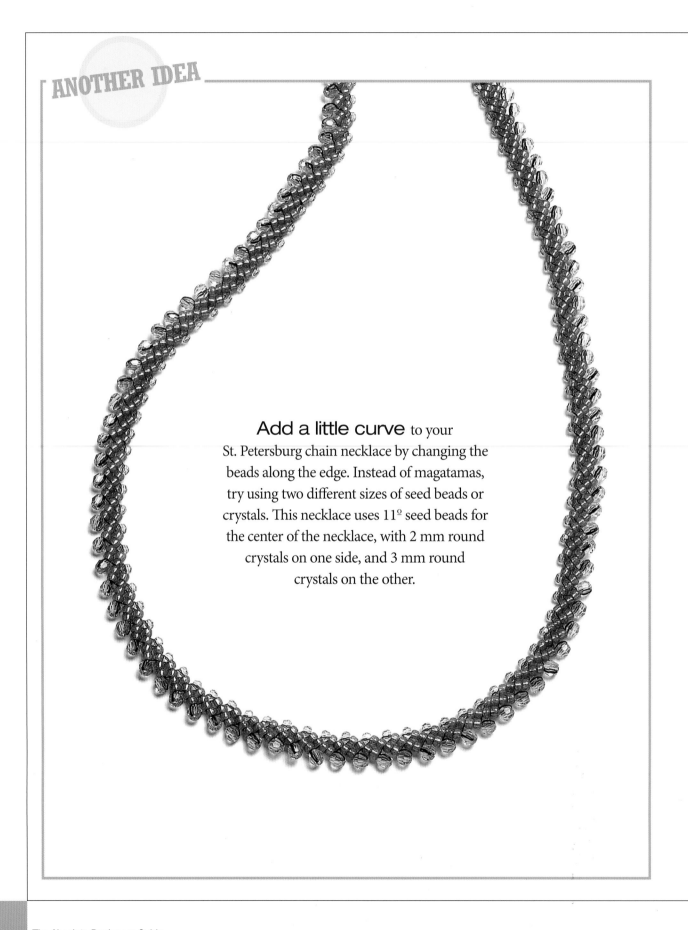

Add a little curve to your
St. Petersburg chain necklace by changing the
beads along the edge. Instead of magatamas,
try using two different sizes of seed beads or
crystals. This necklace uses 11º seed beads for
the center of the necklace, with 2 mm round
crystals on one side, and 3 mm round
crystals on the other.

PROJECT 27

Double St. Petersburg chain bracelets

Create a dressy chevron-patterned bracelet by stitching a mirror-image row of St. Petersburg chain. All you have to do is leave a long tail and sew through the edge beads on one side as you stitch the second row. This simple repetition allows you to create a richly detailed chain, perfect for straps and bands.

Finished length: 7 in. (18 cm)

MATERIALS & TOOLS

- 8 mm clasp bead, round or rondelle
- 31 4 mm bicone crystals
- 5 g 8° seed beads
- 3 g 11° seed beads
- beading thread, size D or 6 lb. test
- beading needles, #12 or 13
- scissors or thread snips

Materials note
To dress this bracelet down for everyday wear, replace the crystals with large seed beads or 4 mm round gemstone or glass beads.

1. Cut a 2-yd. (1.8 m) length of thread, and thread a needle on one end. Attach a stop bead at the midpoint of the thread. (You may want to wind the long tail around a bobbin to keep it out of the way. You'll use this tail to work the second half of the bracelet.)

2. Pick up six 8° seed beads. Sew through the third and fourth 8°s again, so the fifth and sixth 8°s form a second column next to them [**fig. 1**].

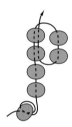

fig. 1

3. Pick up an 11° seed bead, and sew back through the next three 8°s in the column. Pick up a 4 mm bicone crystal, and sew through the two 8°s in the next column [**fig. 2**].

fig. 2

4. Pick up four 8°s, and sew through the first two 8°s just picked up again, sliding the four 8°s tight to the existing chain [**fig. 3**].

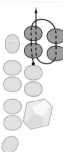

fig. 3

5. Pick up an 11°, and sew back through the last three 8°s in the column. Pick up a 4 mm bicone, and sew through the two 8°s in the last column [**fig. 4**].

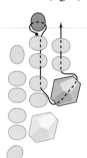

fig. 4

6. Repeat steps 4 and 5 to the desired length of the bracelet. Attach a stop bead to temporarily secure the thread.

7. Remove the stop bead from the starting end of the chain. To add a clasp bead, pick up two or three 11°s, the clasp bead, and an 11°, and sew back through clasp bead and 11°s, pulling the beads tight to the chain [**fig. 5**].

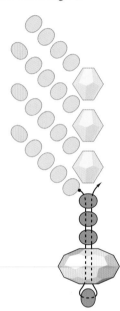

fig. 5

8. Pick up six 8°s, and sew through the third and fourth 8° again, as in step 2 [**fig. 6**].

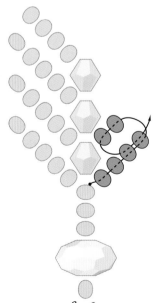

fig. 6

9. Pick up an 11°, and sew back through the next three 8°s in the column. Sew through the adjacent 4 mm from the first side of the chain and the two 8°s in the last column of the second side [**fig. 7**]. Pull tight.

10. Pick up four 8°s, and sew through the first two 8°s again. Pick up an 11°, and sew back through the next three 8°s in the column. Sew through the next 4 mm in the chain and the two 8°s in the last column [**fig. 8**]. Repeat this step to the end of the chain.

11. Remove the stop bead from the first end of the chain. On each side of the chain, your thread is coming out of the last column, which has two 8°s. On one needle, pick up enough 8°s to make a loop around the clasp bead. Sew down through the two beads in the last column on the other side of the chain [**fig. 9, a–b**]. With the other needle, sew through the loop of beads in the other direction [**fig. 9, c–d**]. End the threads.

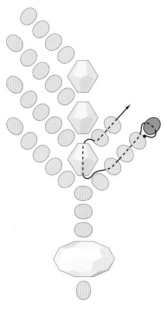

fig. 7

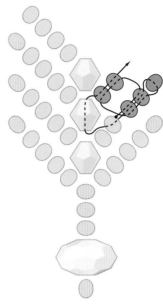

fig. 8

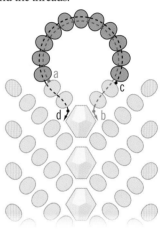

fig. 9

ANOTHER IDEA

Two double chains meeting in a point makes a sleek, V-shaped necklace. You can join the points to a pendant or focal bead by sewing through the hole and ending the threads in the opposite chains.

Stitching terms

Here are some terms that are used quite often in bead stitching. This listing is designed to supplement the visual glossary that starts on p. 10; check that section first for help in identifying commonly used materials and supplies.

AB A rainbow-type bead finish

Add thread To secure a new thread in the beadwork, exiting where the old thread left off so you can continue stitching

Aught A measure of bead width that roughly corresponds to the number of beads per inch, designated by /0 or º

Bead ladder A row of beads stitched together with ladder stitch

Chevron A symmetrical, arrow-like pattern

Core beads In spiral rope, the base beads that other beads spiral around to form the stitch

Decrease Adding fewer beads or stitches to a row than the previous row

End the thread To secure the thread in the beadwork and trim

Fishing line For beading, use gel-spun polyethylene, not monofilament, which can become brittle and break

Gram (g) The standard for bead weights; 1 oz. is equal to about 28 g

GSP thread Gel-spun polyethylene, a strong, synthetic thread

Half-hitch knot A knot around a thread, used to unobtrusively secure a thread

Increase To add beads or stitches to a row

Loop beads In spiral rope, the beads that spiral around the core beads

Luster A shiny finish

Matte A milky, frosted, or non-shiny finish

Nylon thread A common beading thread, available in range of colors

Opaque A solid finish that light cannot pass through

Picot A trim formed by picking up 1–3 beads and sewing through the next bead

Step up To sew through existing beadwork to begin a new row or round

Stop bead A bead that holds beads on a thread; removed later in the work

Symmetrical A design that's identical on each side, also called a mirror image

Thread bridge The thread passing between two beads stitched together

Transparent A finish that light can pass through

Up-bead In staggered stitches, such as peyote stitch, a bead that sits higher than the beads in the row before

Working thread The end with the needle

Zip up To connect two sides of peyote-stitched beadwork by sewing through beads that interlock

Decrease?
Increase?
Bead ladder?

About the author

Lesley Weiss grew up in a family with a strong DIY spirit and has enjoyed doing crafts of all kinds since she was very young. She has been beading since 2003, when she began working for Kalmbach Books. She was the compiling editor for many books in the *Creative Beading* series, had a hand in dozens of other Kalmbach publications, and worked on the staff of *Bead&Button* magazine as well. Lesley enjoys how stitching with beads engages her analytical, puzzle-solving skills and indulges her creative side at the same time.

Lesley holds a bachelor's degree from Washington University in St. Louis and a master's degree in writing from Pacific University. She lives in Southeastern Wisconsin.

Acknowledgments

It always amazes me how many people contribute to the making of a book, and this one is no exception. I am very grateful to the Kalmbach Books team for their work on this book, especially my editor, Mary Wohlgemuth, whose guidance and hard work were essential. Thanks to the art team, including Lisa Bergman and Kellie Jaeger, for the clear and easy-to-follow page layouts and illustrations, and photographers Jim Forbes and Bill Zuback, who made sure the step-by-step photos were clear and the lead shots looked beautiful. I'd also like to thank the editors of *Bead&Button* magazine, who are not only wonderful to work with, but also taught me a lot about beadwork and writing instructions. Special thanks to editorial assistant Lora Groszkiewicz, who helped with some of the stitching, and Julia Gerlach, who made sure the instructions were accurate.

Lastly, I'd like to thank my family: my dad (who didn't really help with the book, but is pretty great anyway), my mom (who did help with the book by testing many of the projects for me, and is also pretty great), and especially my sister, Susan (who tested a number of the projects in this book and put up with the many beads piled on the dining room table, ground into the carpeting, and stuck between the couch cushions).

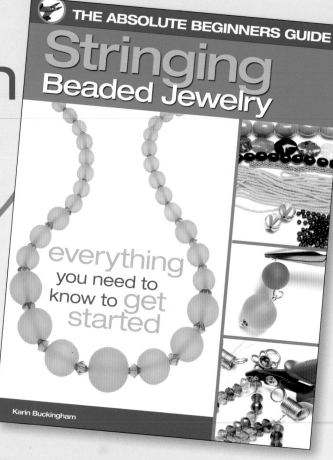
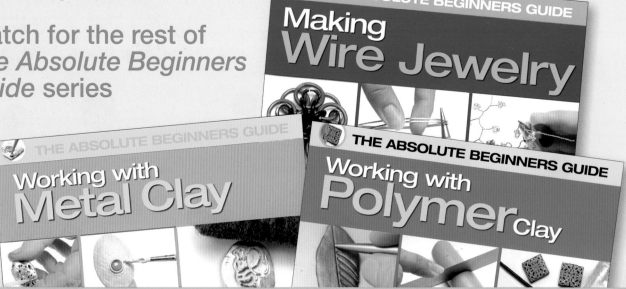